D.lB

POTTERY CRAFT

Noble and original craft
   above all the first,
for in the industry of clay
   God was the first potter
and man the first pot

DISPLAYED IN A POTTERY AT
COIN IN ANDALUCIA

TRANSLATED FROM THE SPANISH

POTTERY
CRAFT

DOREEN
BROOKSHAW

*With line illustrations in the text
by Doreen and Drake Brookshaw
and 16 pages of half-tone illustrations*

FREDERICK WARNE & CO. LTD: LONDON
FREDERICK WARNE & CO. INC: NEW YORK

LIBRARY OF CONGRESS CATALOG CARD NO.: 68–10153

PRINTED IN GREAT BRITAIN BY
WILLIAM CLOWES AND SONS LTD
LONDON AND BECCLES
276.267

Contents

List of Plates   vii

Preface   ix

1 BEGINNING WITH CLAY   1

2 JUST CLAY   11

3 PLASTER OF PARIS   17

4 EQUIPMENT   24

5 BEFORE THE WHEEL   30

6 ON THE WHEEL   38

7 TURNING AND FETTLING   63

8 DECORATION   67

9 GLAZING   82

10 TO THOSE WISHING TO MIX THEIR OWN
   GLAZES   87

11 FIRING   96

List of Ceramic Suppliers   107

List of Plates

1 Neolithic Chinese pot, T'ang Shao period
2 Chinese pottery figure of the T'ang Dynasty
3 *left* Pottery figure, "The Lion Tamer"
  below Stoneware figures, "Vultures for Culture No. 2"
4 *above* Stoneware coil pot and bottle
  below Stoneware pin boxes
5 Earthenware bottle with glass decoration
6 *left* Elegant earthenware work
  right Wine bottle
7 Stoneware bottle and pot
8 Two jugs and a cooking pot, demonstrating the variety of slip decoration
9 Decorated teapot of good design
10 Earthenware bowl, painted and tin glazed
11 *above* Tin glazed group of small figures
   below A fearsome tiger with slip-trailed stripes
12 English slipware plate by Thomas Toft
13 A beautiful dish made at Wenford
14 Thirteenth-century Persian bowl
15 Lead glazed earthenware dish from East Persia
16 Examples of the author's work

Preface

The fact that you have opened this book suggests that you have already an interest in clay or an urge to do some creative work. Clay is a basic, natural material, which lends itself readily to artistic expression. Its very plasticity allows for swift changes of form and texture when expressing an idea. Themes of decoration can be tried and if unacceptable can be erased with a sweep of the thumb. Forms in clay are highly individual, for the hands are in direct contact with the material. The fingerprints of the maker are on every piece. Some beginners may feel shy of joining a class, doubting their own ability, so for them, especially, I have written this book, to help them develop and enjoy this craft. I hope it may also be helpful to teachers starting a pottery class, for all children love clay and do lively work.

Many of the examples among the photographs in this book are classical, and have been chosen for their beauty of form and decoration. If you wish to attain your full artistic potential you should endeavour to develop your taste. This can be done by becoming acquainted with examples of pottery in museums and exhibitions, and as your observation gradually becomes more acute to form and proportion, your own work will improve.

The purpose of this book is to lure you away from mass production, to discover a basic artistic sense. Do not be led away by fashion, for there are fashions in everything, but fashion leads straight back to mass production. Be yourself, and your work will have individuality.

I wish to acknowledge the friendly encouragement and generous help given me by Tony Benham of Mill Pottery, and I should also like to thank Mr Sackman, Head of Putney School of Art, for allowing photographs to be taken at the school.

PREFACE

I am most grateful to all those potters who have been kind and co-operative in allowing me to use photographs of their work. My thanks are due to the Council of Industrial Design for supplying photographs reproduced on Plates 3, 4, 6 (right) and 9; also to the Victoria and Albert Museum and the British Museum for supplying other photographs. The encouragement of my husband has been a great help to me and his many drawings of hands for the poses shown in this book have been invaluable.

El Molino de Las Pavitas   DOREEN BROOKSHAW
Mijas (Malaga) 1966

x

I

Beginning with Clay

There is a joy in the handling of clay, this wonderfully plastic natural material, which has attracted man since the Stone Age. Its appeal lies, perhaps, in its quick response to a creative idea. An apparently dull lump of common clay, some imagination, dexterous fingers, and there may be a work of art, which, when it is fired, could last a thousand years. There are many examples in museums even older than that, yet they are still full of the vigour, enthusiasm and delight of the artist who made them. When we contemplate these works our interest is quickened and the artist no longer seems remote. Clay, then, is our natural inheritance.

You may choose between objects of use or beauty. Ideally, these things should be synonymous, and your best work will demonstrate this fact far better than words.

If you are a complete beginner it will be much easier for you to buy your clay from a supplier. It will be in a good, workable state and is usually sold in a plastic bag, and as long as the bag is sealed it will keep workable. The supplier may also have glazes, which are suited to the clay he is selling, or he will tell you where you can obtain them. Now you are ready to start and get some experience of your material.

However small your space, providing you have one good strong level table you can start. The table surface should be wood or Formica. Some squares of wood or hardboard will be useful because you can put work on them and remove from the table.

The best tools for your first experiments are those you already have, your fingers. There are great rewards awaiting you in the mud pie technique you loved when young. It still holds its fascination.

Take a piece of clay from the bag, roll, press and squeeze it between your fingers. Try rolling it out with a rolling pin. Pick it up, push it

I

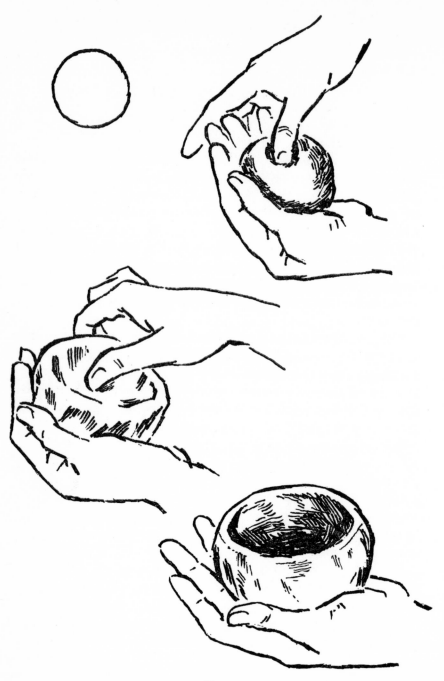

Fig 1

together, bang it down hard on the table to expel the air bubbles. You have first to learn about the feel of clay through your fingers so that you can tell what clay will do and at what point it becomes too dry to work. A damp sponge will soon moisten it. Remember, warmth from your hands will tend to dry the clay, especially if working with a small piece.

When your clay feels in nice workable condition, roll it into a ball. Holding the ball in the palm of your left hand, press your right thumb into the middle of the ball, making a hole. Now try pulling and squeezing up the sides, gradually turning the ball in your palm. Continue turning round and round, pulling up the sides as evenly as you can. Try to make a cup shape by this means (see fig. 1). You may have to trim the top with a knife, but your aim is to train your fingers. It will be good if you can smooth the top with dampened fingers to achieve an even edge without resorting to other means. The Japanese made their tea-drinking bowls in this way.

Another good exercise is building by coils. Pots are still built by this method in various parts of the world. Take a piece of clay, get it into a workable state, roll it into a short sausage shape and lay it on the table. Lay all your fingers on the clay and start rolling it to and fro in order to elongate it. It will seem difficult at first to get it even, but it will come quickly with practice. This is the technique: let the fingers be relaxed and spread a little apart; press lightly but roll quickly, pulling the hands apart as you go to elongate the roll. You will soon be making even rolls. Damp one side of a roll with a little liquid clay and coil it round to make a flat base; or you may roll out a piece of clay for the base, cutting it to the shape you require. Do not make it too thin. Put this on to one of your pieces of hardboard or wood. Now start building up the sides, damping the clay between the coils with more liquid clay. This ensures that the coils are sealed together. There are one or two methods of joining them, as illustrated in fig. 2. See that the joins are well made to be free from air bubbles which might cause trouble when firing.

If you have a definite shape in mind it is a good idea to cut a cardboard template and keep putting it against the outside shape as a guide (fig. 4).

3

Fig. 2 Building by coils

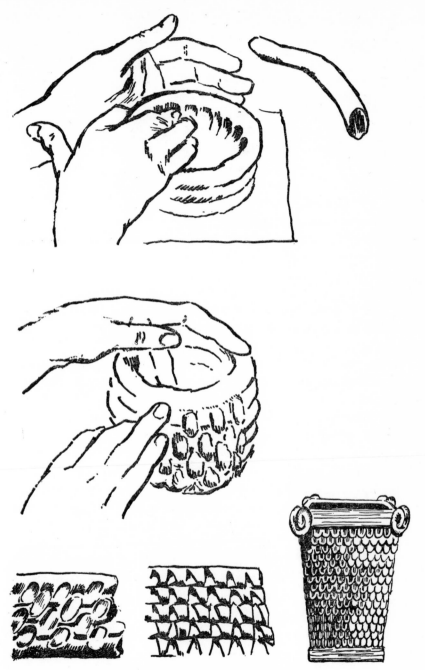

Fig. 3 Smoothing and decorating coil-built pots

It is necessary to draw the coils together to make a strong wall and one
that will fire well; it is also necessary
for a pot to be smooth inside to be
useful, so start smoothing the inside of
the pot when you have added one or
two coils. Draw a finger firmly across
the join of two coils, developing a
rhythmical movement as you turn the
pot, so that the coils are joined
evenly with finger impressions. Now
smooth over carefully, without leaving
small spaces or air pockets. This is important.

Fig. 4

When you have finished the inside to your satisfaction, consider the
outside. You can make use of the coils in the decorative effect of the
outside, by drawing them together in such a way as to form a pattern.
Your finger, or any other instrument, a spoon or knife handle, will do.
Try out one or two patterns by laying pieces left over from the clay
rolls side by side on the table. Then experiment, drawing them together
to make a pattern. When you are satisfied with what you have done,
carry it out on the pot. If you wish, you can smooth the outside as well
and decorate it in some other way. I shall give you many ideas for
decoration in the chapter on this subject. There is no end to the shapes
you can make by this method. It is well suited to shapes other than the
round produced on the potter's wheel. Do not make things too big at
first for remember that you are learning a technique. However, your
pot will shrink as it dries and again when it is fired so you must allow
for this.

When you have tried small cups in the pressed method and built
some pieces by the coiled method, extend your knowledge of clay by
modelling small figures or animals. Your clay must be well wedged or
kneaded. Try to model from a single lump of clay, or build them up
from sausages of clay for arms and legs, etc. These must be well fixed

Neolithic Chinese pot, 2nd millennium B.C. T'ang Shao period. Buff earthenware painted with black and red-brown.
(*Victoria and Albert Museum*)

PLATE I

PLATE 2

The simplicity and dignity of this Chinese T'ang Dynasty figure is a lesson to those interested in making pottery figures.
(*Victoria and Albert Museum*)

Fig. 5 Left and right: Small clay animals from the Messara tomb, Crete
Centre: Greek, fifth century B.C.

together in order to fire successfully, so with each piece that you add, scratch both surfaces and touch with "slip" (liquid clay) and fix firmly together. Make a fine roll of clay and fill the crack, smoothing over with a wooden modelling tool.

Figures or shapes that are modelled very solid can be hollowed out when the clay is cheese- or leather-hard. Hold the piece gently in the left hand and cut out the centre with a tool specially made for this purpose (fig. 6). Try to keep the piece of fairly uniform thickness, in order to be sure that it will fire successfully. These modelled forms should be allowed to dry slowly. It is a good idea to cover them with a plastic bag to exclude the air (no holes in the bag please); tuck the bag under the board on which the modelled

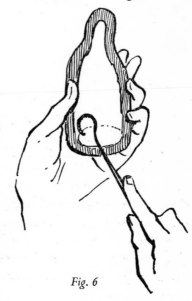

Fig. 6

object stands and set aside in a cool place to dry. Examine the work from time to time to see that all is well. If small cracks appear they can be mended with clay of the same sort, in the same degree of plasticity.

In the illustrations I have given you some examples of modelled pieces. There is plenty of scope for things of beauty and utility, things

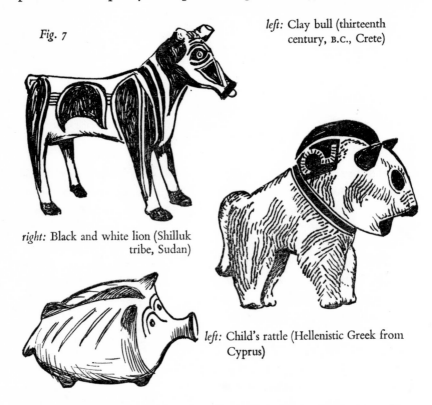

Fig. 7

left: Clay bull (thirteenth century, B.C., Crete)

right: Black and white lion (Shilluk tribe, Sudan)

left: Child's rattle (Hellenistic Greek from Cyprus)

that have the signature of an individual potter. In an era of mass production these objects make an enlivening personal statement.

When making things by hand, you develop a finer feeling for your clay than if you start by learning to throw. For example, your clay must be kept in workable condition. Nothing is more exasperating than having a wonderful idea and then finding that the clay is either too hard or too wet to work. Plastic bags have proved to be ideal for clay storage, but they must be air-tight. Small amounts are sold in plastic containers. Alternatively, you can keep your clay in a bucket with lid, or small dustbin. It will keep moist if a damp cloth is placed on top and a piece of plastic sheeting tucked over it. If it is left too long

Fig. 8

left: Child's rattle (fourteenth century, English)

left: Goddess Giezi (thirteenth century B.C.)   *right:* Staffordshire (about 1740)

and does harden, water must be added, the clay first being broken up to allow the water to percolate; leave for a time to equalise, then work well with the hands until it is smooth. This entails quite a lot of work, so my advice is that you keep your clay in good condition for when you want to work. When you have an unfinished piece, but wish to continue it another time, you must keep it damp, and also the clay with which you wish to continue the work. A plastic bag which is sealed by the weight of the clay will do. Now put it in a cool cupboard—the larder is excellent, if allowed! A biscuit tin is another way of creating a small damp-cupboard. If, in spite of your efforts, your unfinished work does become hard it can be damped again with care. Wrap a damp cloth (well wrung) gently around the piece and cover with a plastic bag as before, and set aside for a day or two.

A proper damp-cupboard is necessary for a lot of work. Any cupboard can be converted by replacing the shelves with open work or slatted material, with a trough of water placed on the floor. If there is an alcove in the room a damp-cupboard can be improvised by placing shelves across the alcove, hanging a curtain across and allowing the base of the curtain to hang in a trough of water. The water travels some way up the curtain, keeping the clay pots behind from drying too quickly. This type of cupboard is more suitable where there is a concrete floor when the trough can be made in the same material.

On the other hand, where work is undertaken in really damp weather or in a particularly damp situation, a drying cupboard is also useful. Any cupboard will suffice that happens to be in a warm situation, for instance, near a radiator or warm pipes. Alternatively, an extremely small electric heater can be placed in the bottom of a cupboard. If you are working alone you will probably find it satisfactory to dry out your next batch of pots by placing them on top of the kiln when biscuit firing.

Now that you have embarked on your experiments with clay, you are free to make many things. After a while, look at the things you have made and judge your progress. If something does not please you, break it up and damp down the clay for use again.

You are working in a medium used by man continuously since the Stone Age. If you are near a museum which has examples of early pottery, do go and study them. Or perhaps you can get illustrated books on Pottery from a Public Library. Try to absorb what knowledge you can of clay and its many uses and note the wonderful variety of shapes and objects. Up till now we have spoken mainly of pots, but ceramic sculpture offers great possibilities, as do tiles which are very useful for trying out schemes of decoration. Enjoy your clay.

Fig. 9 British Bronze Age Pottery

2

Just Clay

Now suppose you are lucky enough to find a local source of clay, somewhere you are able to dig as much as you require. If you are an energetic person this will appeal to you very much. The time taken to prepare it will add greatly to your satisfaction in the finished product.

The clay you buy is really a "clay body", that is, clay which has been mixed with other ingredients to make it suitable for the purpose for which it is intended. What you are about to dig is common clay, inevitably having some impurities.

But first I want to tell you a little about the different types of clay. There are many rocks on the earth's surface. Where these have decomposed and been eroded over thousands of years, clay has been formed. When the clay lies near the rocks of which it is formed it is called "primary clay". China Clay in Cornwall is an example.

Clay that has been carried some distance from its source and has settled finally in large watery beds is very plastic. The Ball Clays of Dorset are of this type. They are so called because years ago they used to be knocked into ball shapes and transported north by pack mules to the potteries.

Clay that has been carried far from its source, gathering impurities, is called "common clay". Of such clay, bricks and flower-pots and earthenware pottery is made. It is very widely distributed and most districts have some. This is the type of clay you will be digging.

Now first make a test to see if you have a useful find. Take a piece of clay and work it between your fingers, picking out any small pebbles. Roll it into a small sausage shape and bend it into a ring. If the outside of the ring starts to crack straight away, the clay is not very plastic and is not worth your while, unless you mix it with some of more plastic type. If, however, it feels and remains smooth and cracks do not appear, you probably have a good close-grained earthenware clay. It may be red-grey, through various shades of ochre, to brown. As a further test, flatten the ring on one side and stand it upright. If it dries without cracking, you indeed have a good plastic clay. If you have not yet acquired a kiln, perhaps you have a friend with one, or the local Art School might help you for it would be very useful at this point if you could get it fired.

A clay that is too plastic will not stand up to tall forms when thrown. This will soon be obvious and can be corrected by adding "grog", which may be in the form of ground, once-fired earthenware pot, fire-clay or red brick. Some sand may also be added—primitive potters used this. These materials can be bought from a ceramic supplier. Grog is sometimes available at brickyards and sand can be dug and sieved to your requirements. It must be freshwater sand.

Your clay when dug will be improved by weathering so leave it outside for the sun, rain, frost and wind to work on it and improve its texture. It should be in a shallow container if it is not to be washed away.

Sometimes, turn it over to expose other surfaces. Be patient, for it will take some months to weather.

When you are ready to prepare it, knock it into smallish lumps, removing any stones, and pour on water. This can be done in any convenient container. Stir and mash it with a stout stick until you have a "slurry". When the clay is smooth and liquid, pass it through a sieve of 40–60 mesh. In a day or so it will be noticed that the clay has sunk to the bottom and there is a layer of clear water on top. This must be siphoned off and the clay left to dry to a workable state. This will be quick if it happens to be sunny. In dull weather, or when wanted in a hurry, it can be spread out on a plaster slab or "bat", as it is called by potters. This serves to absorb the water from the clay. If the clay is left in the sun the hard crust that will form must be turned in from time to time so that it will dry more evenly.

When you feel enough moisture has gone from the clay, roll up your sleeves and work the clay with your hands, breaking up lumps and trying to bring it to an even consistency. If you wish, you may do this with your feet, stamping and treading out the lumps. In Spain, where I am working at the moment, I watched a very old man stamping clay with his heel. He stood in the middle of a heap of clay about 6 ft. in diameter. He worked down the clay, pressing in his heel with a circular movement. When he had finished, the clay lay in a rhythmical dahlia pattern on the hard earth floor of the pottery where he worked. Afterwards it was wedged into large blocks, between which grog was sprinkled. I bought some of this clay for experimenting and was satisfied with its texture.

Now you have a quantity of clay all ready to be wedged. Afterwards it will have to be kneaded, but this can be done before use. It is convenient to keep a good quantity of clay already wedged. It continues to mature in this state and may smell rather strong, but do not worry, for this is all to the good; the bacteria in it are active and its plasticity is increasing.

Wedging is quite robust work and children love to help. You need a good strong table of wood and a wire cutter with a wooden handle

at each end. Take as big a piece of clay as you can comfortably manage, pat it together so that the sides are not too ragged, raise it above your head and let it drop on to the table. Cut it through with the wire, slantwise. Raise one piece and bring it down smartly on the other piece to form one lump again. This must be done with some force to expel air bubbles. Pat together, give a half turn, and repeat. This process is illustrated in fig. 10. Continue in this way until you cut through and find that there are no more spaces or streaks to be seen. This should take about five to ten minutes. If it takes longer it is because your clay is too hard and is wasting your time. Cut it in slices with the wire, put water between and leave for a while, or take some damper clay. A practical fixed wire-cutter for the wedging table can be made with piano wire, as shown in fig. 12.

When your clay is wedged it is ready for kneading (fig. 11). I suggest that you knead when you are about to use the clay. Take rather more than you intend to use (do not run short in the middle of a job). I expect you have seen bread being kneaded at some time; the method for clay is much

Fig. 10   *Fig. 11*

the same. The movement is a rocking one and as you move backward you bring over the edge of clay and rock forward, bringing down your weight on your wrist. The movement becomes rhythmical and the clay works in a spiral shell-like pattern. The clay should feel beautifully smooth and workable. This will take a little time to acquire and most beginners are inclined to skip this. If badly done it will cause air bubbles, so cut your clay and look at it before you start. If, when you are working on the wheel, you hear little popping noises and your clay is thrown out of centre, air bubbles are present and you know

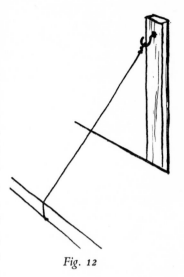

Fig. 12

then that your clay was not carefully prepared. Experience will teach you the difference in really well-tempered clay. It will save many disasters on the wheel.

The common clay you have prepared will be earthenware. This means that it will fire between the temperatures of 900° and 1100° Centigrade and will collapse if taken much higher. Fire a measured bar of clay of about 6 in. and make a note of the shrinkage, which will be important to you if you want to work to size.

Stoneware is a clay which vitrifies, making it hard and non-porous, and is fired at a higher temperature, in the region of 1260°. It is glazed in a different manner from earthenware.

Porcelain is a clay body made from kaolin (white china clay) and other ingredients and is fired higher than stoneware. I suggest that you concentrate on earthenware first. It is in the English tradition and there is infinite scope.

Now that you have clay and have tried it out, you will begin to feel the creative possibilities of your material and the deep satisfaction that it brings.

Slip clay or engobe

Slip clay, or engobe as it is sometimes called, is clay in a liquid state, used for decorating a clay body while it is still damp. If you are going to make traditional English Slipware you will want to know something about the composition of slip.

Slip or engobe decoration is usually done on a clay body of medium tone, so that the decorating slips are darker or lighter in colour.

Dark-coloured slip is easily prepared from your earthenware clay. You let it down with water to a creamy consistency and darken it with the metal oxides of iron, manganese, cobalt or copper. With these you will get warm dark shades to black. Sieve the mixture through a 60 to 80 mesh sieve and it is ready for use.

When you come to prepare a light-coloured slip, there is some difficulty involved. This is because the contraction of the slip must equal that of the clay body, otherwise there will be a flaking of the slip during drying, or biscuit-firing. If you have bought your clay from a supplier, he will sell you a light-coloured slip to equal the clay body. You can colour this with the metal oxides to please yourself. You will have to add a greater quantity of oxide to colour a slip than a glaze, but you will not see the colour in its true value until the fired glaze is over the piece. The glaze will have the effect of deepening the colour, so you can allow for this.

If you have dug your own clay, try using one of the ball clays as light-coloured slip. This you will have to buy from a supplier. The ball clays are very plastic which is necessary to a slip. The colour, however, is buff and to obtain whiteness it is necessary to add some china clay. China clay has little plasticity and the addition must be kept as small as possible so that it is workable. Flint may be added to help fusion and it is also helpful when it comes to fitting a glaze to your work.

The composition will, therefore, run like this: half the quantity will be ball clay, the other half will be made up of two-thirds flint and one-third china clay. Very small amounts of the metal oxides will colour the slip, from 1 per cent to 10 per cent. You will find information on

16

the colours produced by the oxides in the chapter on decoration. Slip clay tends to cake round the sides of the bucket, where dry pieces fall back into the liquid. It will be necessary to keep it stirred and to sieve some before use.

3

Plaster of Paris

Plaster of Paris has various uses for the potter because of its property of absorbing water from clay. For instance, if you have clay in a plastic state but just too wet for throwing, by spreading it out on a block (or "bat" as it is called) of plaster, water will be absorbed. It may be necessary to turn the clay once or twice and knead it gently against the bat to bring it into use more quickly. Very wet clay may be poured into bowls of plaster in order to dry.

Plaster of Paris is also used for the making of moulds. Moulded pottery, however, is not really for the studio potter since it belongs to the world of manufactured ware, where mass production requires such methods. There are some simple moulds which you can make to reproduce shapes other than the round. Your first requirement will be a "casting frame". This is best made of wood and it is necessary to oil it well so that the plaster will come away easily. You can cast against a clean piece of glass placed on an even table, which must also be level. Seal between glass and frame with a good roll of clay. The alternative is a flat bed of clay into which the frame may be pressed. I give you the pattern of an adjustable frame which will serve you well. Fig. 13 will, I think, make it obvious to you. You require four pieces of wood, $18'' \times 5'' \times \frac{7}{8}''$. To one end of each of these attach an angle bracket screwed as shown in the illustration. Take four wooden wedges and assemble as shown in the diagrams.

Plaster of Paris is definitely tricky until you are accustomed to its preparation, so follow the instructions as closely as possible. Plaster

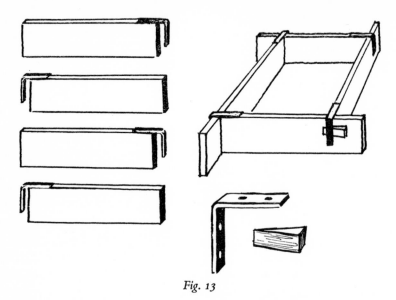

Fig. 13

must be new. Make a point of this when you buy. If it is old there will be a grey scum on the top of the water when you mix it and this plaster never really dries. Consequently, it cannot absorb water from your clay. Store plaster in a very dry place.

Technique for mixing Plaster of Paris

Mix in a large plastic bowl or bucket. The plaster must always go into the water, not the other way round. Fill the bucket with the amount of water required. Measure the plaster in another receptacle from which it can be sprinkled easily and evenly into the water. Do not let it come out in lumps (sieve it if necessary). When all the plaster has been sprinkled into the water, wait for two minutes for the plaster to "slake". This wait is most important. Then start to stir. Put the whole hand in the mixture to the bottom of the bucket or bowl, palm downwards, and stir without breaking the surface as this would cause air bubbles. Another method is to put the hand down with the fingers turned upwards and continue to waggle them until the plaster begins to thicken (see fig. 14).

Fig. 14

When you can draw a finger across the surface and a faint line is left, this is the moment (and I mean the very moment) at which to pour. Pour evenly without splashing. Splashing will cause air bubbles which will weaken the structure of the plaster.

When the plaster has been poured, hit sharply the edge of the table on which you are working. This will bring any air bubbles to the surface of the plaster and these may be dispersed by blowing on them.

The plaster feels warm to the touch as it dries. It sets quickly and the frame can soon be removed. Do not use it for about five days, but allow it to dry right through.

One layer of plaster may be cast on top of another, providing the lower one is still damp. It will adhere completely. If the plaster to which you are adding is old and dry, be sure to soak it well with water and scratch the surface before adding the new plaster.

Recipe for mixing Plaster of Paris

For a plaster bat 12″ × 9″ × 1½″ (or 162 cubic inches)

    2 quarts of water

    5½ lb. of plaster

These are the proportions for a certain amount of plaster; you can increase or decrease them according to your needs. If you do not have scales it is still possible to mix plaster successfully by the following method. Fill your bowl or bucket with water required. Sprinkle in plaster until it shows as a small island above the water. When the plaster has "slaked" its two minutes, pour or siphon off the excess water and mix as usual.

To repeat a shape which will enable you to try out various methods of decoration, it is a good idea to make a mould for a plate or dish of the simple "flop in" type. Make some sketches and decide on the shape. A shallow shape is easier to decorate, and one that cannot be made on the wheel, such as on oval or square, gives variety. You must now model the shape in clay upside down (see fig. 15). If you are working

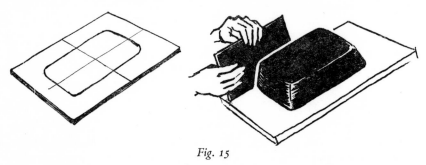

Fig. 15

on a piece of wood or hardboard, mark out the shape in a strong pencil to guide you. Cut a template of the section and keep drawing this along the sides in each direction to guide you into getting the shape symmetrical. When you feel that you have got the shape as perfect as you can, finish the surface of the clay nicely with sponge and fingers. The ball of your thumb is quite helpful for this operation. The dish, which should be damp but firm, is now ready for casting.

Adjust the casting frame to the required size. Remember, the thicker your plaster the quicker the absorption of water from your clay. Therefore, do not make your mould too thin. When you have put the clay model in the frame, make a pencil mark on the side of the frame to indicate the depth of plaster required. The base must be at least as thick as the sides and might well be more. A well-made mould will last you a long time, so it is as well to make it strong. Don't forget to seal outside with clay. Cast by pouring the plaster straight over the clay model to the depth marked on the side of the frame (fig. 16).

Fig. 16

When you have dispersed any air bubbles, see that the plaster is lying flat; if not, pat it smooth with a piece of wood. When the plaster is sufficiently dry, take away the frame. Turn the mould over and pull out the clay. If little pieces of clay remain, take them off with a sponge; do not damage the surface of your mould by digging them off with a tool. The mould must dry completely before re-use. Gentle heat from an infra-red lamp is helpful; too much heat will spoil your plaster.

You now have what is called a "flop in" mould. To fill it, take a good piece of well-wedged and kneaded clay. Roll out with a wooden rolling-pin on a piece of linen, using two strips of wood as a guide to thickness (fig. 17). The thickness of the dish will, of course, be in relation to its size. The moulded dish is best kept a little on the heavy side;

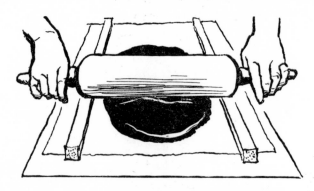

Fig. 17

in any case there will be shrinkage. When a piece of clay rather bigger than the dish has been rolled, pick up carefully with both hands and drop it into the mould (fig. 18). Ease it in gently; do not pull and stretch, for the thickness must be kept even. Sponge it and smooth it as carefully as you can. Trim back the edge with a knife, being careful not to cut your plaster. Smooth the rim and then leave to dry. If, however, you intend to decorate with slip (see chapter 8) this is the time to do it, while the clay is still damp. It will be possible to remove the dish and use the mould again quite soon. I cannot give you an exact time for this as there are too many factors involved: the size of the dish; type of clay; the thickness of the plaster; and the atmosphere of the day. You will soon get to know by experience of your materials how many times in one day you can fill your mould.

Plaster bowls for drying clay can be made by the same method. Any

Left, "The Lion Tamer", by Stanislas Reycham, M.B.E., is partly thrown, partly modelled. This pottery figure has an amusing charm.

PLATE 3

Below, stoneware figures "Vultures for Culture No. 2" by Audrey Blackman. Wit and social comment in clay.

Above, stoneware coil pot and bottle by Ian Auld and *below* stoneware pin boxes made by Tony Gant. Although man has built pots since early times, these examples are very much of today.

PLATE 4

Interesting bottle made by Evelyn Berrisford at Putney School of Art and
described in chapter 5.

PLATE 5

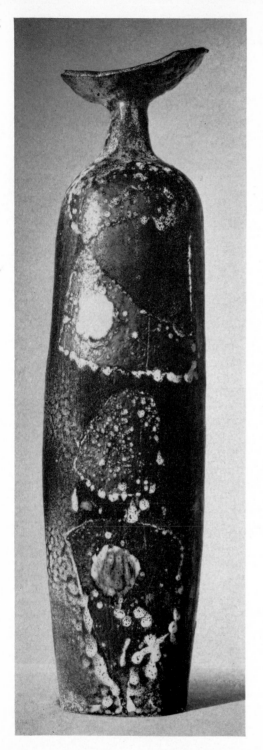

Left, elegant earthenware irregular shape
with intriguing decoration of mottled
glaze and colour patches by Paul Brown
(*Victoria and Albert Museum*) and *right*
wine bottle by Waistel Cooper.

PLATE 6

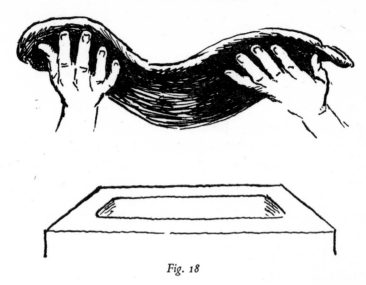

Fig. 18

bowl you happen to have can be inverted for this purpose. A glazed surface will not stick to the plaster; but other surfaces should be lightly oiled.

For a woman alone who feels un-equal to the task of making a casting frame, a strip of lino, tied firmly in a circle and supported by a strong wall of clay, will serve as a casting frame, or cottle, as it is called (see fig. 19).

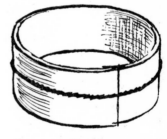

Fig. 19

Final warnings Do not wash spare plaster away down an ordinary sink. Do not get bits of plaster among your clay. It is better to discard clay used in plaster work than to find that it has mixed with your working clay.

4

Equipment

As you become more involved with your work in clay you will want to acquire some equipment. The first thing to arrange is some sort of workshop. Perhaps you have a spare room, an attic, a shed in the garden, or basement space.

There are two necessities—water and gas or electricity. If you are having a sink put in, see that it has a plaster trap; if not, remember my

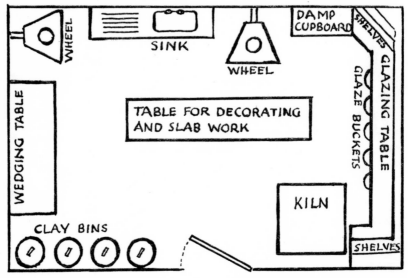

Fig. 20 Plan of a useful workshop

warning not to throw surplus plaster down the sink. Your most important buy will be your wheel. The type of wheel you buy may be governed by the amount of money you can afford. The use of a kick wheel (foot-operated) is the best way of learning to throw, for with this wheel the hands, foot and eye learn to work in unison, the state of the clay is appreciated and great control is learned.

There are models at which you stand and others, rather more expensive, where a seat is provided. I am in favour of a seat for the potter, since he is raised above his clay, which is helpful, quite apart from the tiring necessity of the weight being on one foot. There are models which allow for either foot to be used for kicking and, providing you feel happy enough about changing feet, this would be quite satisfactory.

It is possible to buy a geared kick wheel, by which means you obtain more revolutions to one kick. I have one of these which is good. This type is more expensive than the first mentioned.

It is quite possible for you to build a kick wheel successfully. Try to see a wheel at work first. You will notice how rigid the frame of the wheel

Fig. 21 A kick wheel

remains when working at top speed. The kick bar must be long enough for the potter to swing his leg easily without jerking his body. The seat slants slightly down towards the wheel head so that the potter is well above his clay. The next thing to do is to acquire two wheels, one heavy for the flywheel, about 22 in. or more in diameter, the other about 9 in. in diameter for the wheel head. Wheels can often be picked up in country junk yards, such as wheels from carts or old machinery, or you could cast a flywheel in concrete. A blacksmith would probably help with the crankshaft. The wheel head must have a good, smooth finish and could be of cleated wood or metal. Here is a diagram of the principle of the kick wheel, but do not embark on this unless you are a handyman with an engineering bent.

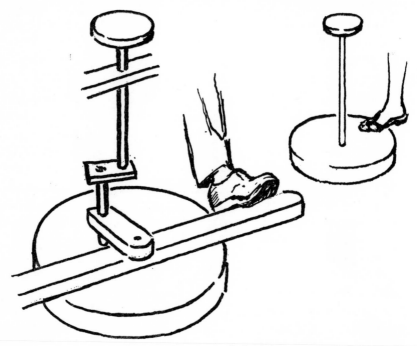

Fig. 22 Two types of wheel drive

If you are a person with little physical energy or time and you wish to produce a number of pots, an electric wheel will suit you better. There are now some quite small electric wheels on the market and the difference in price between the smallest electric wheel and a standard kick wheel has narrowed considerably. The larger electric wheel, capable of taking a greater amount of clay, is much more costly. So you can see that the choice of wheels is wide and you must consider your particular need.

In schools and Colleges of Art it is usual to have a number of each type of wheel. Beginners start on the kick wheel, moving to an electric wheel when more proficient. In the class, those who have been allowed to throw on the electric wheel can return to the kick wheel for turning, thus freeing the electric wheel for others. It is important in a class that there is a fair arrangement of time spent on the wheels.

Your next important buy is your kiln. This is undoubtedly your most vital piece of equipment. After all, ceramic work is possible without a wheel, but it is not practical without a kiln. Do not buy in a hurry, but weigh up carefully the advantages and disadvantages of the various kinds from your point of view. Let the scale and amount of work you intend to produce be some guide to choice.

There is no doubt in my mind that, for the amateur, electricity is the most convenient and cleanest form of heat. Today many studio potters, Colleges of Art and schools use electric kilns. Gas kilns are also very efficient. I have had work fired in a gas kiln belonging to a friend, which was entirely satisfactory. There are some extremely small electric kilns on the market, but these are really more useful for making tests, or ceramic jewellery, rather than for producing pots.

If you are isolated from gas or electricity and a good supply of even-sized wood is readily available to you, it is possible to build a wood-fired kiln. The firing of this is, of course, something that has to be learned by experience. This will give enormous zest to the enthusiastic amateur. Oil and solid fuel are also possible fuels. Building a kiln is not such a technically difficult proposition as might be imagined.

I am speaking now to the handyman. Some of you reading this book may be amateur electricians, or some may feel capable of dealing with gas. Others prefer building a wood-burning kiln. The refractory bricks for the kiln lining, or "muffle", can be obtained from the suppliers mentioned in this book. Those for electricity can be bought already grooved to take the elements. The makers of refractory

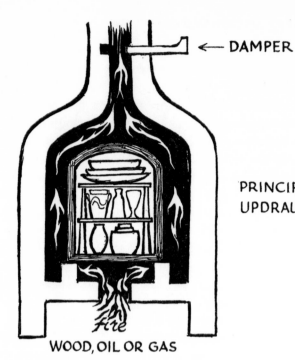

← DAMPER

PRINCIPLE OF THE
UPDRAUGHT KILN

WOOD, OIL OR GAS

PRINCIPLE OF THE DOWNDRAUGHT KILN

Fig. 23

materials will be helpful and your local Gas Board will also be willing to give you advice. If you decide on oil as fuel, then the oil companies will advise. The fuel that will be most difficult to manage will be wood. Only embark on this if you are sure of a good supply of even thickness wood. Relatively few potters today use wood and I advise you to read *A Potter's Book* by that great potter Bernard Leach, who describes and gives proportions for the building of wood kilns.

Whatever method you decide to use, do not make your first kiln too large, nor use the most expensive materials. Experience must be bought in kiln construction, but the making will be full of interest and time cannot be called wasted that adds to one's knowledge.

Other necessary equipment

4 clay bins
Strong wedging table
Plaster bats and/or bowls for clay drying
Bowls, various, for mixing. Bowls with lips are useful for pouring glaze and slip clay
Jugs
Sponges—small fine natural ones
1 large synthetic sponge for cleaning up
Brushes for decoration—Chinese type are good; a liner for banding
1 wide, flat, soft brush for glaze—could be used for slip painting
1 lawn brush for sieving
"Lawns" or sieves, 40, 60, 80, 100, 150 mesh. These are made in different sizes—buy according to your needs
Clay cutting needle
Twisted wire cutter with wooden handles
1 rubber kidney for pressing and smoothing
Turning tools, one pointed and one rounded
1 wire loop tool
Boxwood modelling tools
Kiln furniture according to your needs
1 large flat-bladed knife

1 small pointed one for slab cutting
Cones
Whirler
Callipers (wooden)
Buckets for glazes
Pot gauge
Pestle and mortar
Rolling-pin
Slip tracer
Scales with gramme weights

For teachers wishing to equip a class of students there are economical package deals comprising a kiln, kiln furniture, plastic clays or bodies, glazes, body stains, glaze stains, underglaze colours, on-glaze colours, brushes, bowls, sponges, sundries and potters' tools, of sufficient quantity for twenty students. At least one of these package deals can be purchased for as little as £200.

5

Before the Wheel

Slab building in clay is another method of producing ceramic ware. Building pieces this way is slower than using the wheel, but it teaches so much about the possibilities of clay that it is very rewarding. Potters were producing many fine and beautiful shapes of technical excellence before the invention of the wheel, and following in the tradition will help you to understand your material.

Slab building requires the clay to be handled at different stages in its drying process. The possibilities are appreciated and a rather more precise craftsmanship practised than in coil building. Individual styles are developed when not governed by the round shape of the wheel. By adding handles, lugs or spouts to your built work, you will be trying

Fig. 24   Northern Chinese slab-built head-rest (probably fourteenth century)

out your taste and judgment. Built work is very suitable for classes of youngsters.

For small pieces of built work, your usual earthenware clay will suffice. When you come to build larger pieces, over 12 in. high for instance, the clay must be strengthened by an addition of grog, grog and sand, or some fireclay. Grog is made from biscuit-fired ware that has been ground down and sieved. It can be bought from a supplier in several grades or, sometimes, from a brickyard. You can, if you are energetic, make your own by breaking up your biscuited throw-outs. Put them in a strong canvas bag and hammer them down to a small size. The bag will have to be placed upon a very hard surface to do this successfully. It can be sieved to various grades, between 30 and 60 mesh. The size of grog is naturally in relation to the scale of the work. Alternatively, fireclay can be used instead of or as well as grog. The reason for adding these materials to your clay is for strength. The grog

Fig. 25   Slab-built pot (British Museum)

"opens" the clay, allowing the moisture to escape in the initial stages of firing. Up to 20 per cent or even 30 per cent of these opening materials can be added for large pieces. The grog can be added by rolling out your wedged clay with a wooden rolling-pin; sprinkle the grog all over the surface and bang it in with your fist. Fold the clay twice, roll out and repeat until it appears to be evenly incorporated. Remember, for delicate pieces use fine grog and for large ones, where a texture might add interest, use coarse.

Your table must be very even for rolling out clay for built work. If it is not so, perhaps you have a piece of Formica, a wooden board, or a piece of plain-surfaced linoleum for this purpose. You will also need a good, long wooden rolling-pin, some pieces of muslin, linen or hessian and strips of wood from $\frac{1}{4}$ in. to $\frac{1}{2}$ in. thick and about 1 in. wide, of a convenient length for the work intended. The clay is rolled out on the piece of cloth, using the pieces of wood as a guide to thickness (see fig. 17). The design for the piece to be built must be already worked out on stiff paper or card. The pattern, or template, of the pieces is laid on the clay and cut round carefully with a knife. Take away the surplus clay and leave the sections of your pattern to harden.

The judging of the correct time to join these pieces is one of the lessons to be learned. With a straight-sided piece, it can be left until the leather-hard stage. If there are curves in the design, a little before this stage is advisable. To fix the pieces together, the edges of each section must be scored and touched with slip clay (the same clay as is being used for the piece). Work the edges together until they feel firmly stuck. Now make a thin roll of clay in as firm a state as is workable and fill the crack of the inside join, smoothing in well with a wooden modelling tool. Treat all the joins in this way. Now take the outside corners or joins. Work these together with damp fingers, smoothing to give a slightly rounded corner. This is clay, not joinery, and there seems to be rather a hard, mechanical, unclaylike quality if the corners are too sharp.

For youngsters, a square box with fitted lid is a good first exercise and can be made quite small. They can work out their pattern on paper

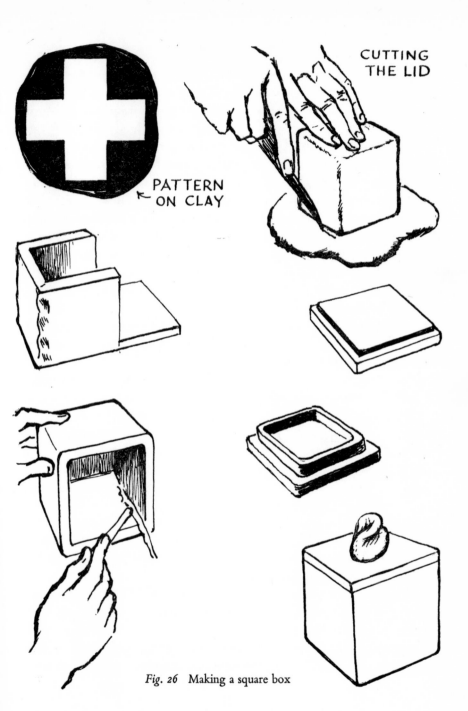

PATTERN
ON CLAY

CUTTING
THE LID

Fig. 26   Making a square box

first, place it on the clay, as shown in the top left-hand illustration in fig. 26, and cut round. A lid can be made out of one piece of clay and a flange cut in it when the clay is hardened or the flange can be added as a long strip.

It will be easier for a beginner to bend up the sides of the box and pinch the joins together on the outside, smoothing and finishing with fingers and sponge; then to insert fine rolls of clay in the inside joins and smooth with a wooden modelling tool. The joining together of leather-hard pieces with slip requires rather more patience than really young pupils are likely to have acquired and may lead to disappointments in the firing. Older students may like to acquire more precise craftsmanship.

Invert the box on to another slab of clay to cut the lid, a trifle oversize. When leather-hard trim to fit, and cut away half the thickness of the lid to form the flange. A flange can be also made by applying a cut strip to the inside of the lid. Make a knob of a comfortable shape for lifting and attach it to the lid.

Slab work does not mean that all sections are necessarily flat. Rounded shapes can be devised by rolling the clay round a cardboard cylinder, or any suitable curved object (see fig. 27). A dusting of flint through a linen bag prevents the clay from sticking to the surface.

Fig. 27

Corrugated cardboard can be rolled and folded into various shapes for supporting clay slabs while drying. With large pieces, the linen for rolling out is a great help in manœuvring slabs of clay and a long-bladed knife is a useful tool for smoothing clay.

The size of the built piece is only governed by the size of the kiln. It is possible to produce a really large piece by making sections which interlock. This could be a project for a class. Another interesting experiment for a class might be a three-dimensional wall decoration, built up from slabs.

Moulds can be used in slab building and the interesting earthenware bottle made by Evelyn Berrisford (Plate 5) is an example. Here, two slabs of clay have been pressed into a shallow bowl mould. These have been joined edge to edge, the neck and foot have been coiled and relief decoration has been made in the foot ring. The decoration has been enriched with coloured glass. Glass has a low melting point and can be used to good effect if broken up and placed so that it has a retaining wall of clay. This bottle was fired lying on its back so that the glass was retained in the shapes allowed. Not all the colours in glass stand up to firing, so fire a sample first before using it in your work. I have picked up glass on the beach and used it—the blues, greens and browns have retained their full colour, but reds and violets lost colour at the temperature at which I wished to fire.

Wash off the salt if your glass came from the beach. A coat of tin glaze behind the glass will show up the colour fully. Slab building is the answer for those who find throwing particularly difficult.

When you visit a museum try to discover how pieces have been constructed; it is an interesting piece of detective work. I have drawn for you a dog of the Chinese Han dynasty, 206 B.C.– A.D. 220 (fig. 28). He is in the Victoria and Albert Museum in London. I decided that his body could have been thrown on the wheel, or made from one slab joined into a cylinder. The head and neck could have been made

Fig. 28

by coiling, the ears modelled and attached; the legs could have been thrown, made from slabs into small cylinders which were afterwards slightly modelled, or they could have been coiled. The tail is a "pulled" handle (instructions in chapter 6). The harness is cut from a slab of clay. He is an interesting and fearsome piece who has bared his cut clay fangs down the centuries, his lead glaze now quite iridescent with time. There is a loving care required of the craftsman to achieve such

a piece, and I feel an affection for this remote and unknown potter when I contemplate his work.

Another drawing (fig. 29) shows a fourteenth-century English jug in the form of a deer. The body has been wheel-thrown, for the ridges made by the potter's fingers are shown in the clay. The head has been

Fig. 29

added, probably with coils. The pulled handle has been modelled into horns and the legs possibly made from clay cylinders, or thrown as shown in spouts for teapots.

Decide what you want to make, then interpret it in the simplest possible terms within the scope of your material.

Fig. 30 Examples of slab work

Tiles

Hand-made tiles can be made by pressing clay into a wooden frame. Fill rather more than full and draw a straight edge over the top to level. The base of the frame should be loose, so that the tile can be pushed out easily. A dusting of flint through a linen bag prevents sticking.

Another method is to roll clay out and leave to harden a little. Then cut the tiles round a template with a sharp knife. Leave to harden a little more and pile them up, with a piece of newspaper between them, to dry. They must be turned over several times in their drying period, to prevent warping. If pieces of newspaper stick, they will be burned off in firing. Clean up edges of tiles with a damp sponge when leather-hard. Hand-made tiles should be kept rather thick. Remember to allow for shrinkage, about $\frac{1}{2}$ in. on a 6 in. tile and an appropriate amount on the thickness.

Fig. 31   Left: Spanish Valencia tile   *Right:* Early English tile

6

On the Wheel

You now have all your equipment in place and are ready to learn to throw. Wedge and knead the largest lump of clay that is comfortable for you to handle. When it is of a nice consistency, cut it into lumps of equal size and pat into balls with the palm of your hand, being careful not to enclose any air bubbles. These will spoil your work when you are throwing. A 10-oz. lump makes a large mug. When you are regularly throwing repeating shapes it will be necessary to weigh out your clay lumps before starting. Line up the balls of clay on the shelf of your wheel or within easy reach. Have your wire cutter, your needle trimmer, sponge and a wooden modelling tool available. You will also need a bowl of water, to which a little of the same clay has been added, beside you on the tray of the wheel. Do not use plain water; the clay becomes "tired" and does not run quite so well; thin slip is preferable.

Damp the wheel head slightly with the sponge and throw your first lump of clay smartly down as near the centre of the wheel as you can. The wheel rotates in an anti-clockwise direction—do not forget this. If you happen to be left handed you may find it easier to rotate the wheel the other way and reverse the hand holds. However, pottery is ambidextrous and, as you are learning something quite new, I do not think those of you who are left handed will find any more than average difficulties.

Throwing

Now, the first thing you have to learn to do is to work that lump of clay to the centre of the wheel so that it is running absolutely true. This will seem difficult at first.

If you are using a kick wheel, start your wheel with a push of the hand in the right direction (anti-clockwise) and start kicking to get up

These two fine pieces are stoneware, chosen to show the refined form obtained when complete control of clay is mastered. The bottle is by Tony Benham of the Mill Pottery, Wateringbury, Kent. The pot by Peter O'Malley is in the Victoria and Albert Museum.

PLATE 7

These pieces demonstrate variety of slip decoration. The left-hand jug, trailed with light slip over dark, is by H. F. Hammond. The right is slip painted by Paul Barron, both from Victoria and Albert Museum. The comfortable cooking pot below is simply decorated with fine lines of slip combed together. Note the strong practical handles necessary to remove a hot pot from the oven. It is by David Eales of Shepherd's Well Pottery, Beaminster, Dorset.

PLATE 8

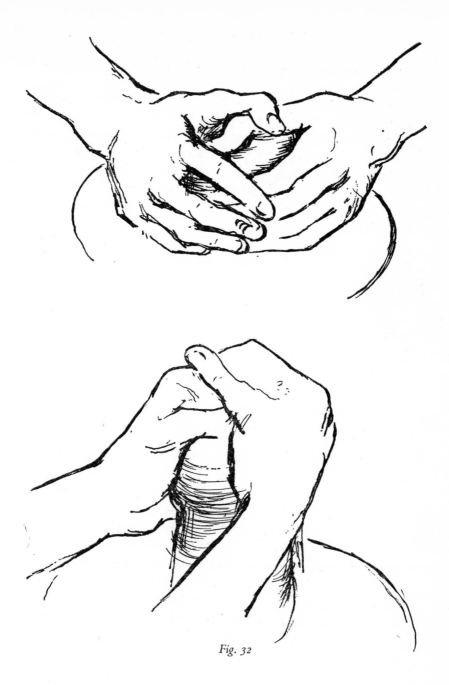

Fig. 32

a good speed. If you are using an electric wheel, switch on and turn to fast.

1 Dip your hands in the clay water, rest your forearms firmly on the tray of the wheel, grasp the clay, your wrists close together, the palms of your hands round the lump, your thumbs crossed on top (see fig. 32, top illustration). Let the clay run through your hands to get the feeling. It may wobble too much. This means that it is not in centre. Your first endeavour must be to correct this. This is the procedure: to make your clay more evenly pliable you are going to work it up and down two or three times until it is the same consistency throughout. It will, at the same time, become centred.

2 Damp your hands, start to exert pressure on the clay and lift upwards (see fig. 32, bottom) to a tall cone. You may have to repeat the movement more than once when beginning. Now the clay must be taken down. There are several ways of doing this—not all potters use the same holds. The one I give you is the one I find satisfactory. Put your left hand round the clay, your thumb on top. Press down with your right palm over the left hand. The left hand is, at the same time, exerting pressure towards the centre. This movement will take the clay down smoothly (see fig. 33, top). Continue the movement till your hands are back to the original position. Bring the clay up and down again once or twice. It is a matter of judgment as to when the clay is nicely consistent throughout. It should by now be centred. At first, you can test it by resting your forearm on the wheel tray and, pointing a finger close to the clay, watch it spin. If there are varying distances between your finger and the clay, you have failed to centre it so far. It is essential to good throwing to be able to centre your clay quickly. As working on the clay proceeds, more water is added through the necessity for damping your hands. Your pot must be completed before the clay becomes too wet, otherwise it will collapse. You can see, therefore, that the sooner your clay is centred, the more time you have in hand and the longer you can experiment with changing the shape of your pot on the wheel.

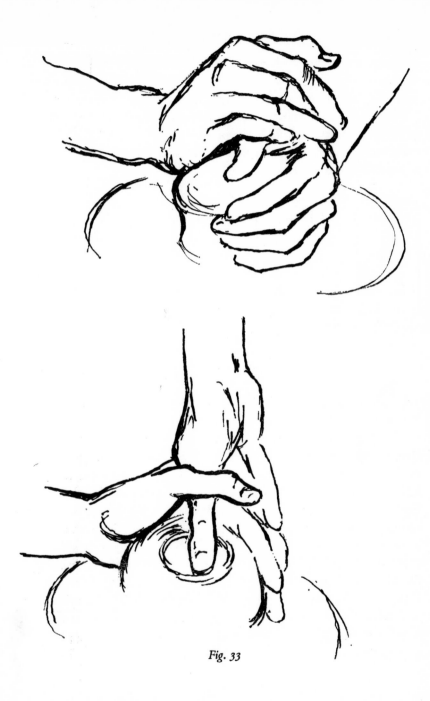

Fig. 33

The first exercise in clay is to be able to throw a cylinder of even thickness. This is the basic shape from which all tall shapes are afterwards formed. You must be prepared to put in a lot of practice on this. It is best to be quite ruthless with your first pots and cut them through to examine them carefully for even throwing (fig. 34). When you can throw a really good cylinder you are well on the way to producing a set of drinking mugs.

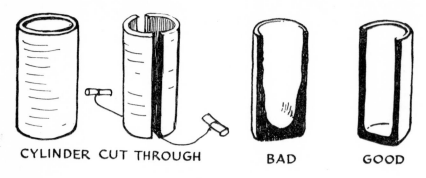

CYLINDER CUT THROUGH   BAD   GOOD

Fig. 34

Let us return to your lump of clay spinning centrally on the wheel. It is now time to open out the clay. Slow your wheel somewhat. I think fig. 33, bottom, is self-explanatory. The left hand is round the clay, the right thumb presses down in the centre. Do not press down too far but leave a base for your cylinder. Note how the hands are locked together; increase pressure with the right-hand thumb to open. Fig. 35, top, is a steadying movement. You will not need this if your opening out has been perfect. However, any tendency to wobble will be corrected with this hold.

Fig. 35, bottom, shows a first lifting movement. Note again the way the hands work together.

Fig. 36 Change to this lifting movement to bring the cylinder to its full height. The inside fingers of the left hand are opposite the bent knuckle of the right hand. The thumb of the left hand is braced against the right hand; this ensures an even thickness.

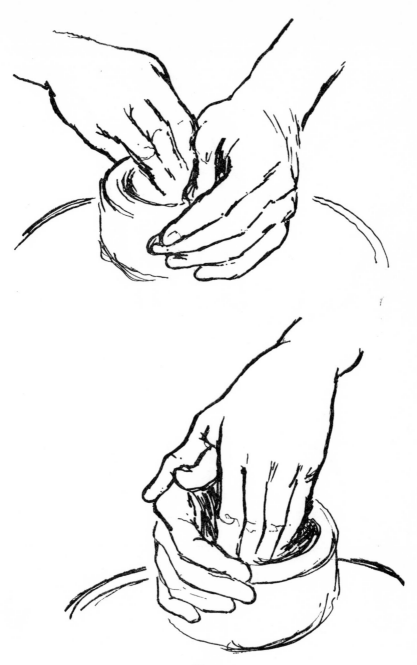

Fig. 35

Fig. 36

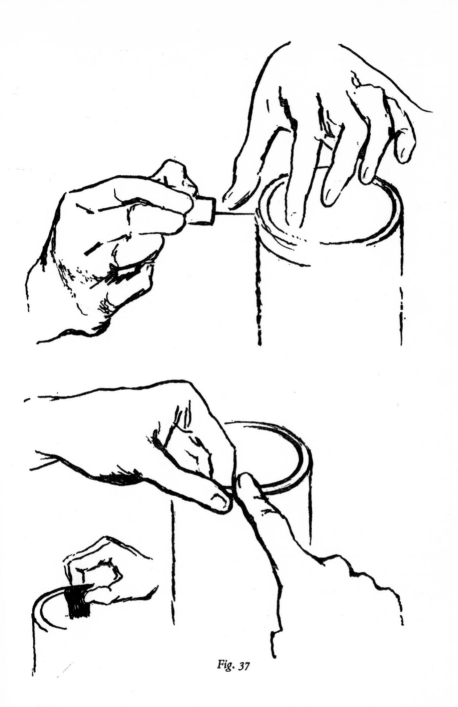

Fig. 37

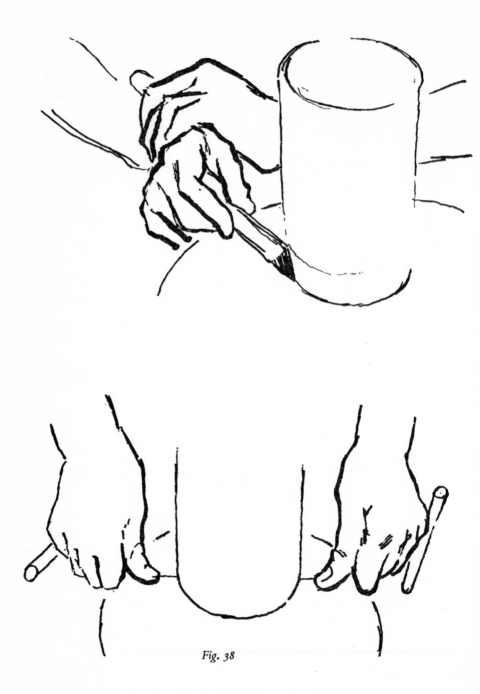

Fig. 38

Fig. 37, top   If the top of your cylinder is uneven, cut it with the needle stuck in a cork. Resting your forearm firmly on the wheel tray, dig the needle into the revolving clay. With a deft movement of the left hand remove the cut strip.

Fig. 37, bottom   Smooth the cut edge with a damp finger, supporting the top between the first finger and thumb of the left hand. A better finish to the edge can be given by using a piece of damp wash-leather, as shown in the small drawing.

Fig. 38, top   Revolve the wheel and, supporting your right hand with your left, clean up the base of your cylinder with a tool, cutting through the clay to the wheel head. Clean up the wheel head with the sponge.

Fig. 38, bottom   With your wire cutter you are now going to remove the pot from the wheel. Stretch the wire taut by pressing down with your thumbs and let it pass under your pot, close to the wheel head.

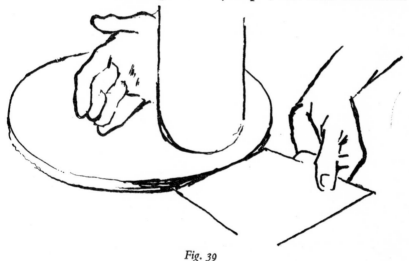

Fig. 39

Fig. 39   Damp one side of the wheel head with your sponge. Also damp a square of hardboard. Slide the pot off the wheel on to the board, using the base of your palm on the base of the pot. If you distort it, do not attempt to correct it by touching the top at this point. It may

47

settle back but, if not, it is much easier to correct when drier. Put aside to dry to the leather-hard stage, when it will be ready for turning.

Throwing is, to some extent, a matter of confidence once the principles have been learned. Some beginners tend to become exasperated with their clay; their muscles become tense and their throwing is doomed to failure. Your wheel speed, the clay and you must be in unison. The clay will rise easily without physical effort from you, if it is of good consistency and your hold steady and confident. Any effort to force the clay to rise quickly, with too strong a hold, will cause the pot to spiral and, if pressed too far, it will collapse.

Fig. 40

There is a point I would like to make here. A cylinder of clay can only be pulled up as far as the structure of that particular clay allows. If you wish to throw a very tall pot it may be necessary to alter the structure of your clay, strengthening it by the addition of sand and grog, or fireclay. In Granada I have watched old men throwing the big water jars which are in daily use in the town. These wonderful old craftsmen produce 18-in. high jars with small necks and strong handles. The ease with which these jars rise is wonderful to see, and one is produced every few minutes. They are stood on boards in rows in the sun to dry, and a man comes out of the pottery with a rope of clay in his hands and attaches the handles to the still wet pots. His touch is sure and expert. I have drawn one of these jars to show you (fig. 40) for I consider them a beautiful shape. They have a long tradition behind them. Such a jar is pictured in Velasquez's painting "A water seller of Seville".

Single-handed throwing

Single-handed throwing is possible for small pots. The clay is centred with the right hand. The thumb depresses the centre and opens

48

out the pot. Pressure between thumb and fingers raises the pot; the right hand must be supported at the wrist by the left hand to bring it up steadily as the clay wall is thinned. A thickened rim gives a slight emphasis to the finished pot and helps to strengthen it.

Shaping

When really good cylinders have been mastered, shaping can be practised. Trying to achieve beautiful shapes before you have enough control to throw a good cylinder is not the way to become really competent. Look again at fig. 36. With this movement, the pressure of the index finger (or first two fingers on a larger pot) inside and the bent

Fig. 41

knuckle of the right hand outside, the shape of your cylinder can be altered to suit your taste. The most difficult shape to form is a full-bellied one with a small neck. Try making the full shape first. When making your basic cylinder see that you keep a thick wall of clay at the top. It is necessary to keep some clay in hand so that you are able to complete the shape for nothing is more annoying than to reach the neck and find that you have run out of clay. Naturally the cylinder you use to practise shaping will be thicker than those you have been making as cylindrical pots. Exert pressure on the inside finger or fingers and bring out and upwards, letting the knuckle outside follow and steady your hold. When you can no longer rest your forearms on the tray of the wheel, try keeping your elbows into your sides for strength and rigidity.

The neck of the pot must be brought in by the movement called collaring (fig. 41). This is a gentle inward and upward movement which must be made slowly or you will get a spiral ripple. It can be corrected if it is not too bad, but great care is needed: the clay must be supported on the inside by the left hand, while the right hand repeats the collaring movement on the outside until it is smoothed out.

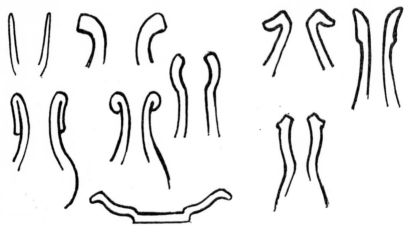

Fig. 42 Rims

Attention must be paid to the rim of the pot (fig. 42). There will be a tendency to split if it is allowed to become too thin. It is better to be sure to have a little clay in hand here. It can always be trimmed with the needle in the cork if it is uneven. Smooth the rim and thicken a little. An emphasis at the rim seems to stop the upward growth of a pot.

A jug is a simple piece of shaping to try first. The making of a lip and the adding of a handle can be tried at the same time. This is pictured for you in fig. 44. Making a lip that does not allow drips to run down the jug is quite a challenge to the potter. See that the inside finger is taken down far enough inside the jug. The rim must be strong enough to allow the pulling out of a lip, which is a strain on the clay. The finger must be damped and the clay stroked gently, supported by the

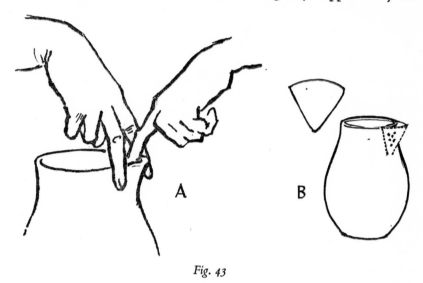

Fig. 43

first and second finger of the other hand (fig. 43, A). Sufficient over-hang on the lip will prevent dribbles, but it does not always look well. Another method is to cut a V-shaped piece of clay and attach a lip with slip and modelling tools (B).

Pulling handles

A handle must be made of the same clay in the same state as the jug. When you take the clay for your jug, always put aside a piece to be used for the handle. It needs to harden a little. Your jug is now on the

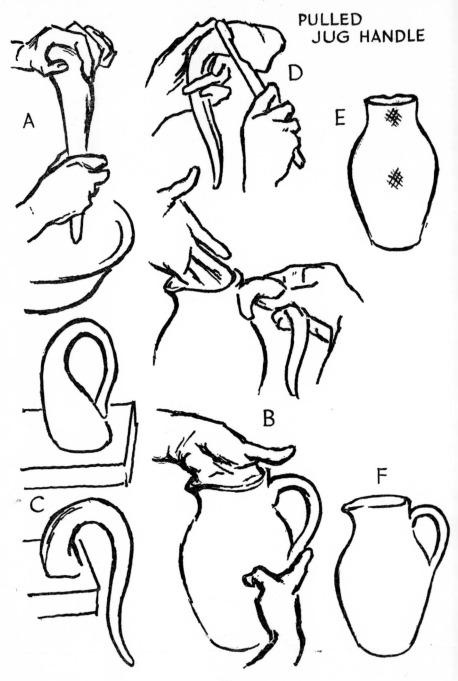

PULLED
JUG HANDLE

A

D

E

B

C

F

Fig. 44

wheel, the lip is made, the base has been cleaned up and bevelled with a tool. You can now attach the handle. Take the piece of clay you have put aside, and hold it over a basin of water or the sink. Damp one hand and pull with a stroking movement, repeated again and again until you have a tapered rope of clay (see fig. 44, A). Do not attempt to do it too quickly or it will break. You will find that there are several possible sections you can make just by the way you place your fingers, and it is fascinating to try out various holds. When you are satisfied with your handle, nip off with thumb and fore-finger the length required. Mark a spot on the jug directly opposite the lip, score it lightly, touch with slip and press the top of the handle in place, supporting the wall of the jug from inside with the other hand (B). Press out the ends of the handle on to the jug with your fingers, making two or three strong, simple strokes. These can be left as a decorative feature if well arranged. Remember a handle must be part of the whole shape of your jug. It needs to grow simply and strongly out of the shape, so the way it is attached is important.

Perhaps it is easier, as a beginner, to attach the handle at the leather-hard stage. If you feel this, remove your jug from the wheel when you have made the lip and finished the base. Pull the handle and let it fall over in a natural curve supported by the extra clay at the thick end (see fig. 44, C). Put aside to harden. When you come to attach the handle cut through the top surplus clay of the pulled handle (see fig. 44, D) and try the shape against the jug. Make any adjustments you feel necessary. The handle can be damped a little with a sponge and gently coaxed until you are satisfied with the shape. Place the handle against the jug and draw with a modelling tool round the points of contact. Rough up the clay at these points (E), also on the handle. Touch these points with slip and attach firmly, supporting from the inside with the other hand. Smooth in the joins and, if necessary, fill in any cracks with fine rolls of clay pressed in with a wooden tool.

The judging of the weight and shape of a handle is all-important to the overall shape of the jug. You must allow comfortable space for the fingers and the handle must be strong enough to lift the jug when full.

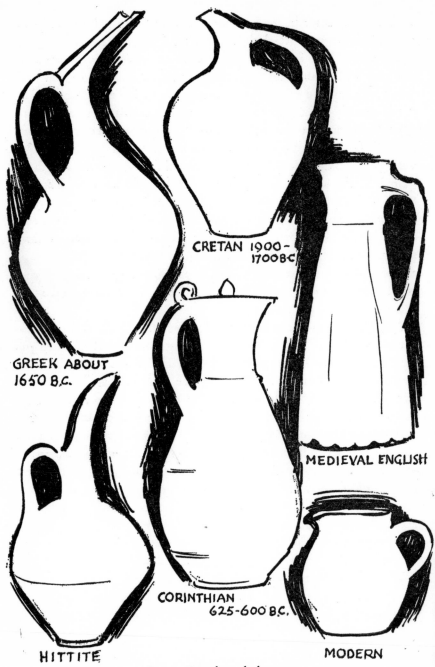

CRETAN 1900 – 1700 B.C.

GREEK ABOUT 1650 B.C.

MEDIEVAL ENGLISH

HITTITE

CORINTHIAN 625 – 600 B.C.

MODERN

Fig. 45 Jugs through the ages

Teapot by Horlock Stringer. There is a good feeling of rhythm about this design. The spout is high enough to allow the pot to be filled fully. The handle leaves room for the lid to be easily lifted. The simple decoration is satisfying to the whole shape.

PLATE 9

Earthenware bowl by Steven Sypes. It is impressed and embossed with a trumpeting angel. Painted and tin glazed.
(*Victoria and Albert Museum*)

PLATE 10

The handle seems to fit most practically and usually most gracefully over the concave curve of a jug (F). I have drawn some jugs of different periods to show you what I mean (fig. 45).

As your throwing im-
proves you will be anxious
to repeat shapes and sizes.
You will have already
done some practice in this
with cylinders. An adjustable pot gauge is a useful
thing to have for measur-
ing the height and width
of repeated shapes. A
handyman can easily make
one. I have pictured one
in fig. 46. A pair of
wooden callipers (mine
are home-made) and

Fig. 46 Pot gauge

a strongly marked foot rule are all you need. Weigh your clay and pat into balls of equal size for repeat work.

Fig. 47 Types of mugs

Throwing open shapes

Now that you have had some experience in throwing, fig. 48, top illustration, will be self-explanatory. The pressing in with the heel of the right hand, while the left supports the clay on the outside, is an

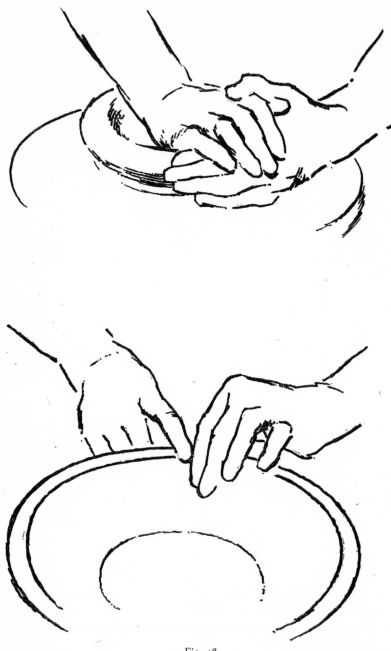

Fig. 48

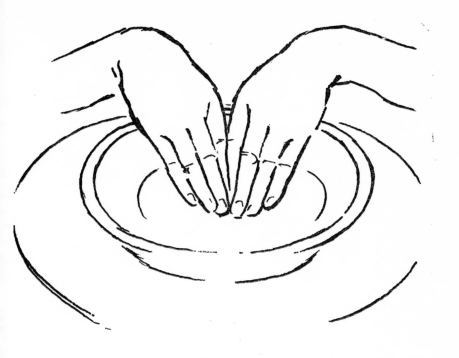

Fig. 49

opening action that can be used for plates or shallow bowls. The throw-ing of a plate with a rim augurs a nice control of the clay. The inside surface must be smooth if it is to be comfortable to eat from and a wooden rib tool is more efficient than the fingers. I have, however, shown one smoothing action of all fingers together, drawn firmly from the centre outwards (see fig. 49, top).

The thick rim of clay at the edge of the open shape can be drawn upwards for a shallow bowl (fig. 49, bottom) or up and outwards for a plate rim (fig. 48, bottom). Very large plates suitable for decorating with slip can be made on a bat so that it is easy to remove them from the wheel without damage.

Bats are made from cleated boards and can be bought or made. Rounds of asbestos or plaster will do. To attach the bat, thump out a coil of clay on your dampened wheel head. Flatten it with a turning tool. Damp the clay, place the bat on it and hit it with your fist. It will attach itself, but make sure you have it centred.

To make the plate take a good lump of clay and drop it on the dampened bat. Hit it with your fist as the wheel revolves, gradually working outwards, until you have a flat disc of clay with a very thick rim. This rim can now be lifted up and out, but do not work on it too long; the state of the clay must be watched for plate rims have a tendency to collapse. Clean up the surface of the plate with your sponge and fingers, rib tool or rubber kidney. If you are going to decorate with slip, this can be done now. The bat holding the plate can be prised off the wheel head and another put in place.

A Teapot

It will be some time before you are sufficiently practised to attempt a teapot (fig. 50). It is a difficult thing to achieve since it has all the problems. The lid (thrown upside down), the pot, the spout and handle must all be made at the same time and put aside to harden, when they must be joined together with meticulous craftsmanship. What a challenge to your skill!

Throw the body of the teapot as you would a vase, starting with a cylinder and shaping suitably. Bring in the top and form the seat for the lid. This must be accurate and a piece of wood with a square end will do this well (fig. 51, A). When really skilled you will do this with your fingers. See that the walls of your teapot are evenly thrown and not too thick.

Fig. 50

The spout is thrown as a small cylinder which is pulled up and in-wards. As it gets higher and smaller, put a wooden modelling tool, or pencil, in the top to keep it from becoming too small and to smooth the inside (B). Cut off the wheel as shown in C and put aside to harden.

The handle must be pulled and allowed to harden.

The lid must be thrown upside down (D). The knob can be turned from the thick underside of the lid when leather-hard. The lid must be held in a "chuck" (see page 65). You must measure carefully the opening of your pot with the flange of your lid. Use callipers for this. Make the flange deep to prevent the lid falling out when the pot is tilted. When both are quite dry, you can put the lid in the pot and turn it, so grinding it to a nice fit. Do not make it too tight; remember it has to be glazed.

The holes to keep back the tea-leaves must be made after you have trimmed your spout to the right length. The length of your spout is very important; it must be as high as or a little more than the pot itself, otherwise the pot cannot be filled completely without spilling. Try the spout against the side of your pot and mark where it will be attached. Draw round the shape with a tool. Allowing for the thickness of the

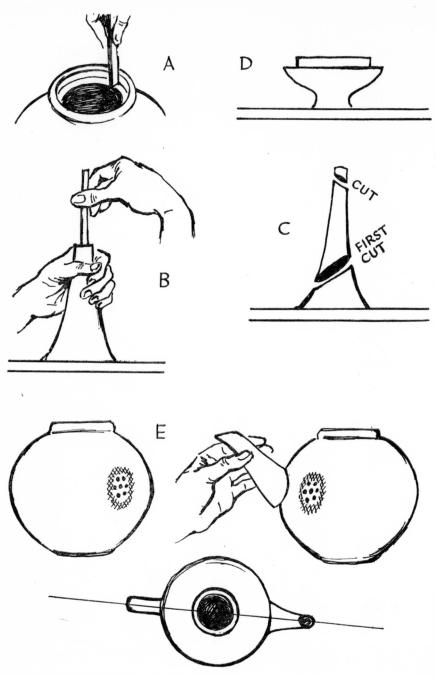

Fig. 51

wall of the spout, make your holes within this shape. A piece of umbrella spoke makes an excellent instrument for this operation; it takes out the piece of clay as it makes the hole. Shave down the wall a little before making the holes and see that you make enough to pour well.

Try the handle against the side of your pot and adjust it to balance the spout nicely.

Now you are ready to assemble them. Rough up the clay with cross-hatched lines on all the surfaces to be joined (E). Touch each surface with slip and press together well. Smooth in the joins with dampened fingers. When you have made sure of the fit of the lid, put it in place and set aside to dry, unless you intend decorating your teapot with slip.

Points to remember when throwing

1 Practise centring, the wheel going fast.
2 Practise cylinders, cylinders and yet more cylinders, slowing the wheel to raise.
3 Wedge and knead your clay well. If you hear small, popping noises when throwing, these are air bubbles bursting. Your clay was not well enough prepared. It may be thrown out of centre.
4 If you come across a piece of rough grit in your clay on the wheel, dig it out and fill up with clay equally wet.
5 If you detect a wobble in the clay you are working, try to steady before continuing.
6 Your whole body works when throwing, your eye, hands and foot.
7 Give a strong rim to pots to prevent warping when they are drying.

Lids

1 A lid needs to be thrown at the same time as the pot so that the leather-hard stage is reached by both pieces and the fit can be assured at this stage. The first one pictured in fig. 52 is thrown the right way up, the knob being included in the throwing.

2 This is a cover to a jar, thrown upside down and afterwards turned to a smooth top.
3 An inset lid thrown upside down, the knob being turned in the thick underside when leather-hard.
4 This is an inset lid with a flange, thrown upside down, the knob being made from the thick underside.

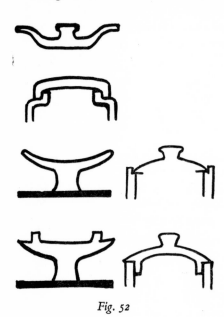

Thrown or modelled knobs are, I feel, more attractive than the mechanically turned knob. There is, however, plenty of scope here. After turning a knob, the lines can be softened by damp fingers or a sponge to give it a more clay-like quality. If you are going to model a knob, remember that the lid and the knob must be of the same consistency when joined, otherwise, in the shrinkage of drying, the knob may become detached. Looped handles can be made from pulled pieces of clay, as you have been shown with jugs.

Fig. 52

Make sure the ends are well worked into the lid. Handles must be considered as part of the overall design of a piece. They must, at the same time, be extremely practical. Roll out a sausage of clay and give yourself an idea of weight and shape required before you start to pull your handle. Handles can be cut from a straight strip of clay, shaped and left to dry a little before fixing.

Casserole handles are sometimes thrown hollow and attached (see fig. 53, A).

Lugs, or ears, are small strong handles as pictured, attached for lifting. They are pulled and are often triangular in section. They have been used on the sides of cooking pots down the ages. Here are some examples:

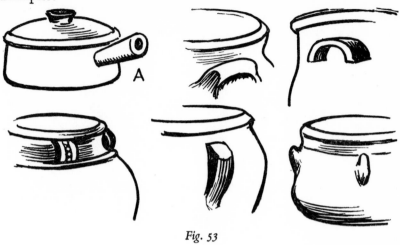

Fig. 53

Feet

Feet can be made by scoring the base and pressing on pieces of clay which are then modelled with damp fingers into the required shape.

For a very heavy piece feet can be thrown shaped and then the end closed, so that the foot is hollow. The fixing is achieved by scoring and attaching with slip.

7

Turning and Fettling

When your thrown pots have reached the leather-hard state, take them off their boards and examine the bases. These will need cleaning up by trimming, or "turning", as it is called. The tools for this work are

63

called "turning" tools and they are illustrated in fig. 54. Some are double-ended, but about three tools are enough for you at this stage. Most people have a favourite tool which they tend to use more than the others. Keep the tools sharp or they will not work well for you.

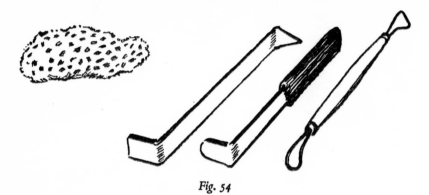

Fig. 54

Your pot must be centred on the wheel upside down. The experienced potter does this with the wheel turning, tapping the pot with the base of the palm of the hand. Do not try this yet—it will probably be fatal. Most beginners find this re-centring of a pot on the wheel very difficult. Some wheel heads have concentric circles marked on them and this makes it easier. If yours is without these, here is a suggestion. Take a sponge with some slip in it and go across the wheel head, leaving a thin layer of slip. Take a wooden tool, rest your right forearm on the wheel frame and, steadying your right hand with your left, touch the wheel head with the tool; swing the wheel and a circle will be clearly marked on the wheel head. Taking this as your guide, you will soon have the pot perfectly centred. You may find that your pot is not quite as round as you supposed: in this case centre your pot as nearly as you can. If you are a person to whom this is a great aggravation you can endeavour to correct it in this way: take an object that you know to be mechanically round (such as a jam jar) and about the same size as your pot and very gently twist it in the top of your pot. It cannot be done if the edge is thin and too dry or it will split. An alternative and, I feel, a more imaginative approach is to change the shape of the top of the pot. This is achieved by taking the pot in both hands by the foot and tapping it gently on a flat surface until you have made a shape other than round.

When your pot is centred on the wheel, it must be fixed with clay. Usually three lumps are enough to fix it firmly. This is for a round pot. If you have a shape with a small neck, or any shape that will not balance well when inverted, it is usual for a ring of clay to be thrown at the same time as the pot, to support it when being turned. This supporting clay holder is called a "chuck". Dust the chuck with flint before fixing your pot so that it will not stick.

How much you have to shave away from your pot is determined by the thickness of the base you have left. A jug, for

Fig. 55

instance, is usually taken well down to the wheel head when thrown and only needs cleaning up slightly and chamfering the edge to bring it to more even thickness.

A bowl will need a foot ring to be cut (figs. 55 and 56). The turning tool is held firmly in the right hand, the thumb uppermost. The fingers of the left hand rest lightly on the turning pot. Make a vertical cut on the outside to the depth intended for the foot ring. Shave off a little below to neaten. Make another vertical cut for the width of the foot ring. Now start to hollow out the centre. Do this from the centre outwards. An eye must be kept on the thickness of the pot. A tap on the base of the pot will tell you the thickness when you have had a little experience; it is not unusual for a student to cut through the bottom of a cherished pot—so be careful.

Fig. 56

Turning is the final statement about the shape, so please examine the pieces you intend to turn and see if it is possible to improve them at this stage. Do not carry the turning too far, for it is desirable to keep the vigour of the thrown marks of the potter's fingers on the pot, otherwise it will appear mechanical. Balance must be looked for. Finally, clean up the base of your pot with the sponge and put aside to dry.

When all your work has been turned, look over it carefully and see that it is well finished. Check that handles, feet and lugs are adhering; if not, fill up cracks with fine rolls of clay of the same consistency and smooth with a wooden tool. If the top edge is rough, it may be smoothed with glass paper. Do not overdo this; it is a remedy, not to be used without cause. As your technique improves you will not need such aids.

The time your pots will take to dry will vary according to the thickness and the atmosphere. A pot may dry out completely and yet take up water again if the atmosphere is damp. There is less likelihood of distortion in drying if it is done slowly. If you have a warm cupboard, you may finish the drying process in this before firing.

8

Decoration

To some of you this part of pottery will be the most enjoyable, to others the most intimidating. If you have had very little artistic experience you may not feel very confident. Do not feel dismayed. Some of the most beautiful effects are obtained with great simplicity.

The object of decorating a pot is to enhance the appearance. If you feel that the shape alone is satisfactory, restrain any temptation you may have to add unnecessary decoration. The glaze will be enough. Paleolithic man, I am sure, really enjoyed decorating his pots with incised designs achieved simply by his finger-nails. Sometimes he pressed in cockle shells and later twisted cords. Some of his designs have great refinement and really enrich his pots.

Painted decoration on pottery needs confidence and a bold approach. Working on a rounded object has its own difficulties, apart from design. Let your first attempts be deliberately simple. I feel there is a lot to be learned by decorating in the raw state with the material itself.

Fig. 57 Cretan storage jar

I saw, in the island of Crete, the great storage jars made for the palace of Knossos. These fine pots (some 5 ft. high) are decorated in many different ways by the application of rolls of clay which are impressed with the thumb of the potter in rhythmical patterns. These jars, dating from about 2500 B.C., are an example of relief decoration executed with simple good taste. There are similar jars on the island of Rhodes, which have been incised. These are made of a deep red clay and the shadows in the incising give a rich all-over pattern.

Perhaps you have already tried some clay decoration on your pinched or coiled pots. Try adding some clay-worked decoration to a thrown pot and notice the character it adds through changes of texture. For instance, small medallions can be cut out of clay, designs impressed on them, and these attached to the pot. Score the clay where they are to be applied, touch with slip and press well against the

68

pot. This can be done at the leather-hard stage. The medallions must be of the same degree of dampness as the pot if they are to adhere satisfactorily. Medieval jugs were often decorated in this way.

Incised decoration

This should be done at the leather-hard stage. Use an ordinary lino-cutting tool for this. The V-shaped one will do. Have a clear idea of what you intend. You can design it on paper, but do not try to trace it on to the clay; this is the coward's way. You must be bold and it is better to start this way. Mark, very lightly indeed with a pointed tool, your design on to your pot. Consider every line as you place it. It will not come as it did on the flat paper; you have to learn to design on the round, which is why I say do not trace. Engrave your design which should be fairly simple. For instance, much crossing of lines is to be avoided; too much of this and your surface may become rutted and untidy. The character of engraving is that the design is made by the shadows and it is better kept simple and clear-cut.

Inlay

This is an extension of incising for, in this case, the design is first incised and then the engraved lines are filled with clay of a different colour. The second clay must be in a softer state than that into which it is being laid. Push it well into the incised design and leave a little standing above the surface. Put aside until the inlaid clay has become harder, when the whole surface can be scraped down to reveal the design more clearly. Use a sharp knife for this. It may be necessary to scrape a second time very delicately, for no stains of one clay upon another must show in the final result. Many early English tiles were decorated by this method. You may see some in the Victoria and Albert Museum, London.

Decorating with slip (engobe)

First try slip-trailing. This is done directly on to the damp clay, rather like icing a cake. In fact, if you have had experience in doing this, slip-trailing will come more easily to you. Today a rubber bulb with tapered glass tube attachment is sold for slip-trailing (fig. 58, B), but the old peasant potters of Staffordshire made their own of biscuited

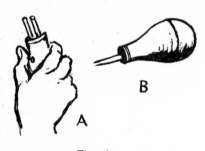

clay (A). They were made to fit comfortably into the hand. One hole, from which the slip trailer was filled, was stopped by a cork into which one or two goose quills were fitted. This was the working end. Higher up was another hole over which the thumb fitted. The thumb controlled the flow

Fig. 58

of slip. You may care to try to make one like this. Alternatively, if you are used to folding and using an icing bag made of waxed paper, you will find this easier.

It is essential in slip-trailing to have the slip of the right consistency and it is advisable to sieve it before use, as smooth running is essential. It should be slightly thicker for trailing than for dipping.

Designs must be extremely direct and should be tried out on a piece of waxed paper if you feel unsure.

It is possible to sponge off if you wish to change what you have done, but remember that freedom is the spirit of this type of decoration. Do try to see some of this work done in the seventeenth and eighteenth centuries by British peasant potters, such as the Toft family (Plate 12). Their work will delight you with its strong sense of design

Fig. 59 Slip-decorated tea-caddy

and naïve drawing. Black and white slips were frequently used with clear amber glaze. There are traditional patterns made with the trailer which you may care to try. One is called "feathered ware" (see fig. 60). This is usually done on to a flat slice of clay which is afterwards dropped

Above, this tin glazed, blue decorated group of small animated figures has all the charm of fantasy. It is by Wilfred Gibson of Falmouth. *Below*, this fearsome tiger with slip-trailed stripes is the work of Linda Hammond aged 13 years, a pupil at Lavender Hill Girls' School, London. Note the lively freedom of the slip-trailing.

PLATE 11

English slipware, richly decorated by Thomas Toft.
(*Victoria and Albert Museum*)

PLATE 12

into a shallow mould of a plate or dish. It is easier to handle if the clay has been rolled out on a piece of hessian or coarse linen on a wooden board. Damp the rolled-out clay with a sponge. Pour on the background slip and drain off. While the surface is still shiny, trail parallel lines of a dark-coloured slip across the surface. If the board is lifted a little and allowed to drop back on to the table, the lines will flatten slightly, but will not mix. Now, with the end of a dampened pointed feather, draw lines across at right angles to those trailed. If you like you can do this to and fro, or in one direction only. You will be surprised how, by this simple means, a pattern of delicate lines is made into a wonderful all-over design which could not be achieved by any other method.

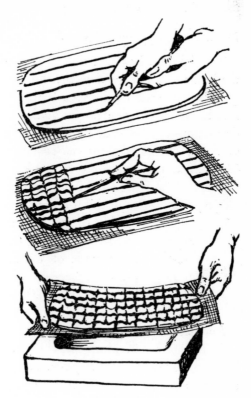

Fig. 60

Let us suppose that you have been not very successful with your first attempt, the lines being rather erratically trailed. Try shaking the board and twisting it this way and that, which will give a marbled effect that can be quite pleasant. This, however, is a matter of luck. Blobs of slip may be formed at the top inside edge of a bowl. These will run down towards the centre, where they can be spiralled by twisting the bowl.

These methods of decoration are technical and require a certain dexterity which most of us can learn. It is in the choice of the colours of the slip, and knowing when the design is complete, that your artistic faculties are called upon.

Decorating by dipping in slip

The slip must be rather thinner than for trailing. If you wish to slip the inside of a pot, pour in the slip, swill round and empty. Do this quickly; you must not let your leather-hard pot become too wet. Pots may be held with spread fingers inside and dipped to the rim. Interesting decorations can be made by just dipping the rounded sides of pots in slip. Any unwanted drips can be taken away with a damp sponge. Slip may be painted on the wet or leather-hard ware, but it must be done boldly with a well-loaded brush and thickly applied if it is not to disappear in the firing. A broad band of contrasting slip painted on to a wet pot can be given a running design with a comb-like instrument made of wood, leather, or a piece of thick rubber (a piece of an old tyre would do). The wheel is revolved and the hand worked up and down. It can be done with the fingers alone, to good effect.

COMB

Fig. 61

Another simple form of decoration which can have great character is the cutting out of simple shapes in thin paper. These are damped and stuck to the leather-hard clay pot. The pot is dipped in slip. As it dries, the paper can be peeled off and the design is left in the body colour. Some metal oxide colour can be brushed on around the design before the paper is peeled away, to give a richer effect.

Wax resist

In principle this method is similar to the last but the effect is different because, by using a brush, finer work can be achieved. Liquid floor wax is excellent for this purpose. With a brush (keep old ones for this use) paint freely a design on your leather-hard ware. Dip in slip. Where the wax has been painted, slip will not settle and you have a design in the colour of the clay body. The wax burns away in the firing. This method of decoration is attractive in that individual styles seem so varied. It is not very easy to paint with the wax; freedom and a bold hand are called for.

Sgraffito

This means scratched, and here the design is scratched out of a coating of slip to reveal the colour of the clay beneath. Great variety is possible. Large masses may be scratched away, or thick and fine lines only may be used. The work can be done when the clay is damp but firm, or when it is dry.

When scraping damp clay (for which wooden modelling tools are best), do not remove the curls of clay immediately. They will dry and brush off later without damaging the surface.

For working in dry clay, a sharper instrument is needed: an old thin penknife whose blade you know, a sharpened wooden paint-brush handle, or a nail file. You must find an instrument that suits you. The character of the decoration in the damp clay is different from that in the dry: that done in the damp clay has greater freedom.

If you are decorating a plate with a light-coloured slip, pour in the slip and empty. Clean up the edge with your sponge. An interesting variation can be made by freely painting some patches of colour with one of the metal oxides and then sgraffitoing the design through the slip and colour. There are many fine examples of sgraffito work in the Victoria and Albert Museum in London. If you cannot visit it, per-haps your local museum has some pieces. Try to see examples of the decoration in which you are interested; it will open your eyes to the possibilities.

Painted decoration

A pot is abstract. That is to say, when you throw you do not have in mind a shape taken from nature but are trying to create a shape beautiful in itself. This shape must also be appropriate to its function. Decoration, then, must enhance the shape already achieved. If it is an extension of this shape it will create a harmonious whole. Do examine the pot on Plate I. This Neolithic Chinese pot of the Yang Shao period (second millennium B.C.) has been beautifully decorated. The broad sweep of its bold brush-work flows rhythmically round the full top shape. Where the neck comes in, the scale of the brush-work has become finer to suit the smaller shape. A running waved line goes round the base of the design as a finish. The portion left undecorated is equally important to the whole design. There is a lesson here: the shapes left are as important as those put on; this is the essence of good design. Your taste will develop as you work and study the best examples.

Fig. 62 Cretan water jar

You can give yourself some idea of your intended decoration if you put it on paper, but it is much more difficult to execute it on a rounded surface. This needs confidence which will come with practice. Use your throwouts for practising brushwork. It is desirable to have a whirler for decorating. It is essential for "banding", that is, putting lines or bands of colour round pots (see fig. 63). Take a brush loaded with colour and, steadying your elbow on the table, put the brush against the pot, whirl it with the left hand and there is your line upon the pot.

The brushes themselves are of primary importance (see fig. 64). It is also necessary to know which sort of strokes each brush can make. You must be quite familiar with your tools to be a good craftsman. There is no need to buy too many brushes at first. Banders (B) have long bristles so they can carry a load of pigment. A wide, soft, square-ended brush is necessary for large areas and also for applying glaze. The Chinese calligraphic brushes (A) are very good for variety of line. The

Chinese were great wielders of the brush for everyone who could write did so with a brush, and the results were highly skilled works of art. Other beautiful brush-work was done by the Moors in southern Spain. I advise you to see, if you can, the bowls and plates of Hispano-Moresque pottery at the Victoria and Albert Museum; or you could send for a

Fig. 63

small booklet on them. There are several booklets on pottery which, at the time I write, cost only 2s. each; they will be a source of inspiration to those of you who are not within reach of museums. Do not look for inspiration among manufactured pottery; there is so much that is bad, and hand-work is a thing of the past. Designs are mostly applied by transfers and are often unrelated to the shape they decorate.

Recently in Granada I watched two young girls and a woman decorating plates by hand. They were working in a long tradition. The speed and taste exercised continually was wonderful to watch. They appeared to have two or three designs by heart. However, these never came exactly alike, since they painted directly on the bisque with their colours of cobalt and copper oxides, ground and mixed with a little glaze. There were birds and leaves and flowers, no two exactly alike, but always well balanced, for every stroke was in relation to the one that had gone before so that unity was always achieved in the final

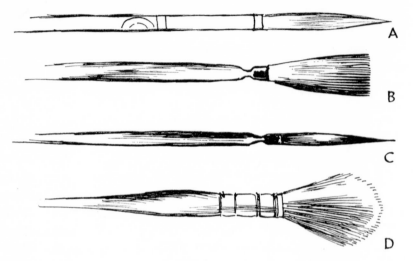

Fig. 64 Brushes: (A) Chinese calligraphic (B) Bander (C) Majolica pencil (D) Goat-hair mop

result. This is a point I want you to remember: once you have committed yourself by one stroke on a pot, the next must come in relation to that one, the third in relation to the two. In this way, the design is built up until you feel it to be complete. At first, aim at great simplicity. A few well-chosen strokes are often enough to decorate a pot. Another approach, if you like rich design, might be to cover one of your pots with bandings, and abstract patterns between, in order to try every possible stroke with your brushes. It would be an exercise in taste. Be bold; don't be afraid, for you will learn a lot from your mistakes.

Underglaze painting

This is best done on a light clay or over light slip, since the colours, if painted on a strong red iron-bearing clay, are naturally dulled by the

76

ground colour. A clear glaze is usual, or a clear glaze tinted with one of the oxides. The raw mineral oxides may be ground on a piece of glass with a palette knife, using the same amount of glaze which will act as a flux. It must be the same glaze as is used afterwards over the ware. When these materials have been ground to a smooth paste, this can be thickened with treacle or gum arabic, let down with water as required. Work must be done very directly with bold strokes, with no going back over your work. If a mistake is made it must be sponged out quickly before the colour has seeped into the surface. These colours may be painted on to the raw ware at the leather-hard stage, if preferred.

Commercially prepared underglaze colours can be bought. These have some advantages, since the materials have been fritted (fired together and ground).

Underglaze painting can be done at the leather-hard stage or on biscuited ware. The source of colours for the decorations on pottery are the metallic oxides. They do not obey the rules that you have known in other forms of painted decoration. These metallic oxides are melted by heat and may produce a totally different colour from that which you paint on the surface of your pot. There are a considerable number of these oxides, but there are only so many in general use by the potter. You must begin to know these metal oxides. Some oxides will produce very different colours according to the temperatures at which they are fired.

If you feel that this all sounds very difficult, do not hesitate; go and buy ready prepared underglaze colours. Mix them with water with a palette knife on a piece of glass and start decorating. These colours should be stable so you will know just what to expect. A clear glaze is usual over underglaze colours, or it could be a clear glaze tinted with a little metal oxide or glaze stain. There are some beautiful examples of early Persian earthenware, painted in a blackish-green colour, covered by a clear turquoise alkaline glaze. The clay of these pieces is pale buff. What simplicity! What a wonderful effect! On the other hand, if you have an interest in chemistry or if you are a person who wants to really know your materials by finding things out in the manner of the early potters, you will enjoy experimenting with metallic oxides. Do not buy too many at first. The oxides must be ground well with a palette knife on glass with an equal amount of the same glaze that is to be used to cover the ware. When you have reduced it to a really smooth paste, add a little gum arabic or a solution of treacle and water, until it is easy to manage in the brush. The design can be indicated in pencil —it will disappear in the fire. Now tackle your decoration with directness, one stroke at a time. Do not go back and try to touch up. This will show in the final result. Do not allow the colour to pile up or this will look unsightly through the glaze. Some beginners imagine that the glaze will hide mistakes—they will learn that these are, unfortunately, accentuated by it.

Here are some oxides which I suggest that you should try. The number listed in the suppliers' catalogues is formidable. Start with a few; experiment and record the temperatures at which they were fired. Make yourself some small tiles of light-coloured clay and some covered with white slip for this purpose. This will give you an opportunity to try out strokes with your brushes.

These are some of the most useful oxides: iron oxide, copper oxide, cobalt oxide, chrome oxide, nickel oxide, antimony oxide, manganese oxide.

Iron oxide This colour is present in all the earthenware clays. Even though the clay looks grey in its natural state, it will fire to a terracotta colour. Iron oxide, therefore, gives warm colours of buff, tan and red according to the quantity used and the temperature at which it is fired.

Copper Gives greens with boracic or lead glazes and, used with an alkaline glaze, will produce turquoise.

Cobalt oxide This is a tremendously strong blue. You may find it easier to use cobalt carbonate as it is more even in colour. Manganese added to cobalt will give deep purplish colours according to the proportions.

In its raw state cobalt oxide is pinkish-grey in colour and this makes it rather difficult to imagine the finished design, since it does not show up on the light body of your pot. You will be amazed at the strength of colour when fired. The edges of the design may tend to flow in firing and a slightly blurred effect may result. This can look attractive.

Chrome oxide is a most versatile performer. You can experiment considerably to see what your kiln can produce. At temperatures of 875°–905° C., with a lead glaze low in alumina, bright orange and red are possible. If your low-fired lead glaze contains some soda, a brilliant yellow can be achieved, providing the temperature is low. With glazes fairly low in lead and without zinc oxide, chrome will give a rather heavy green; with copper oxide, more attractive greens. Chrome with tin oxide present can give pink or brownish-red. If lime is present, violets, browns and greys are possible. Here is a field for experiment. The factors are proportions plus temperature. Good, clearly defined brush-work is possible with chrome.

Nickel oxide This may not be considered a very attractive colour by itself, being a warm greyish-green. Used with iron oxide, it is helpful in producing various browns.

Antimony gives yellows and these are best in combination with lead glazes.

Manganese This oxide is most frequently used with iron for strengthening the tones of browns and blacks. Without iron present, small amounts used with boracic and lead glazes will give cream. With some lead glazes a rich purple-brown can be obtained. Alkaline glaze plus manganese will give violet.

You will get tremendous interest out of your experiments with the use of oxides. There will be great satisfaction in trying to understand your materials. Do take careful notes of your experiments. It would be exasperating to have a wonderful result that pleased you and be quite unable to say how it was obtained.

Suggested percentages for colour combinations of oxides for earthenware.

COLOUR	OXIDE	PERCENTAGE
Brown	Rutile	5
	Manganese	5
	Iron	3–7
Black	Cobalt	1
	Iron	8 }12%
	Manganese	3
Red	Pink chrome/tin	5
	Coral chromium (with high lead)	5
Tan	Rutile	2
	Manganese	2
	Iron	2
Yellow	Uranium	5–10
	Tin-vanadium stain	3–6
Green	Copper oxide	1–5
	Nickel	3–5
Blue	Cobalt	$\frac{1}{2}$–1
	Turquoise copper (alkaline flux)	3–5

% here represents an amount to colour a glaze

Majolica decoration

Majolica decoration is done on the unfired opaque tin glaze. I prefer to paint while the glaze is still damp. I prepare the oxides beforehand so that I am ready to start when the glaze surface is dull but still damp. However, this may not be convenient to you and you may be faced with dry glaze with a powdery, difficult surface on which to paint. A thin coat of gum tragacanth can be brushed or sprayed over the piece. I have been told that some sugar or molasses mixed with the glaze gives it a harder coat, when dry, for painting, but I have not tried this. Your brushes are most important. Brushes that hold a full amount of colour, but will go to a fine point, are good (see fig. 64, c). You cannot use pencil for indicating your design because this would spoil the surface of your glaze which should be a nice, smooth, even coat to receive your decoration. You can put down the main lines of your design in indian ink applied with a brush. This will burn out entirely. This is also practice with the brush for the final work, which should be done freely. Ceramic brushes are long-haired in order to hold enough colour. You may feel at first that they are difficult to control. Practice will help. They are made not to be held too close to the working end, but further down the handle, so that you can see more of the whole design as you work.

There is a very wide range of hue in the prepared majolica colours which you can buy. Do not buy too many at first. Remember the pleasing effect of Chinese blue and white ware, or the Dutch Delft and some English Bristol.

If you are using the raw oxides, please be very light-handed with cobalt which is extremely strong in colour. If too much raw oxide is used, a dark metallic quality will result. Colours may be painted one over the other.

Your decoration will melt, to become one with the tin glaze. The colours will have depth and a translucent quality not possible with other means. Everything is possible in majolica—it is up to you to find what is desirable. The fine brush-work of the Chinese and the Hispano-Moresque will show you the approach to painted decoration. The Italians, so clever in the arts, gave way to florid decoration in this field, having a painter's, rather than a potter's approach.

Overglaze enamels

These are painted on after the ware has been glaze-fired. They are not often used by studio potters except, perhaps, for lustres. They are really the equivalent of low-fired coloured glazes and require a further firing at $830°-875°C$.

There are a whole range of colours obtainable for this work and I suggest you buy one or two if you wish to try this. It does make available a wide range of colours but, as I have pointed out to you already, artistic excellence is not dependent on an abundance of materials.

Be good to your brushes. Wash them well after use and coax them into points and stand them on end in a jar. If you are not going to use them for some time, wrap them up and put away carefully, for moths love them!

9

Glazing

The shelves of your work-room are now full of biscuit-fired pots decorated with slip, resist, sgraffito and underglaze painting. Now comes the final stage, that handsome, glassy covering that adds to the beauty and use of your ware—the glaze. It is the most important stage in the whole process. It can also be the most tricky. The opening of the kiln after a glaze firing is the culmination of, perhaps, weeks of work for the potter. Just as the make-up of the ware and firing are variable, so glazes can be temperamental. The opening of the kiln can be the most exciting and wonderful experience, or the most exasperating and disappointing. Attention to detail, well-applied glaze and careful packing of the kiln, will help towards success.

As I mentioned at the beginning of this book, if you have bought your clay from a supplier, you should ask him to supply or tell you where to obtain a glaze to "fit" the clay body he sold. That the glaze should fit the clay is most important. By using the prepared glaze and firing it to the given temperature you can be reasonably sure of a good result. You will then be able to contemplate your first batch of completed pottery and judge for yourself the results of your work.

I am presuming that you will be working in the earthenware temperature range of 1200°C. and under, probably 1060°–1100°C. Do not buy a great number of prepared glazes, but try working within limits set by perhaps two: a clear glaze which will look well over your slipware, sgraffito and underglaze-painted pots; and a majolica glaze which will give you an opportunity to practise on glaze-painted decoration with metal oxides or majolica colours bought for the purpose.

Even with these two glazes great variety can be obtained. For instance, the clear glaze can be stained with very small amounts of metal oxides, or bought glaze stains. One glaze can be tried over another— this is best applied to shallow shapes or bowls. With a combination of underglaze or slip painting and tinted clear glazes, many rich effects can be obtained. If you buy the minimum of materials and work with them until you feel you have exhausted the possibilities, you will have purchased a large amount of experience very reasonably. I say this because, when I look through the catalogues of ceramic suppliers, the variety of glazes seems endless and it would be possible to spend a great deal of money to no greater artistic success. Most of the really beautiful ceramic pieces of the past were made with a few basic earthy materials. The potter of the time understood his materials and worked simply and directly within the limits set by them. The really noble pots of the Sung and T'ang dynasties in China illustrate what has been achieved with these basic materials.

The technique of glazing

First, I am going to tell you about the technique of glazing. Later I intend to explain something of the nature of glaze for those who wish to experiment in mixing their own.

The prepared bought glaze is mixed with water to a cream-like consistency. Buckets with lids make good containers, for dust and other oddments fall into glaze which is left uncovered. It is as well to keep glazes stirred, since the heavy particles fall to the bottom. Mix completely before use and pass through your finest bronze wire sieve, or lawn as it is called (100–150 mesh). A brush for this action is called a lawn brush. Be careful to mark your buckets clearly so that you know what is in them. Do not mark the lids only if these are interchangeable, for confusion may arise.

If the biscuit-firing of the ware has been low, the porous nature of the pots tends to absorb the glaze quickly and smoothly. In classes for beginners this is an advantage since there is a certain deftness to be acquired with glaze application for it to be successful. The higher-fired pot is more difficult to glaze but is more practical in use. If a pot is very dense and hard and difficulty is experienced in glazing, it can be dipped in water first. Wait until all the moisture has gone from the surface before applying the glaze.

Pots may be dipped, or double dipped into the glaze, which must be of sufficient depth to cover them. Glaze may be poured, brushed or sprayed. To glaze the inside of a pot, pour in glaze, swill it round and empty. Any drips can be removed with a damp sponge. For the outside, invert the pot on two pieces of wood over the glaze container and pour glaze quickly over the pot from a jug (see fig. 65, top). Studio potters do not, as a rule, glaze the foot of pots as this is an added complication when firing. Clean up the base carefully, for about $\frac{1}{8}$ in. up the side, with a wet sponge. This is to allow for some spreading of the glaze.

Turn the pot right way up when sufficiently dry and examine the edge. The glaze is dry and powdery and any lumps can be smoothed down by rubbing gently with a finger. If the glaze is incomplete where the pot had been in contact with the wood, touch in lightly, one stroke at a time, with a brush full of glaze. If preferred, the sponge can be run round the top edge, which is left bare as a decorative feature.

If a different colour is to be used inside, glaze the outside first. Should there be drips left from pouring out the inside colour, remove these carefully with a razor-blade knife when the glaze is dry.

Double dipping takes practice, but it is well worth acquiring the dexterity (fig. 65, centre). Take the pot firmly by the foot with thumb and fingers, dip into the glaze and press down with a jerk, lift (not free of the glaze) then dip again, twist each way quickly to ensure covering the inside. Withdraw and allow to drip before standing on its foot. It is more helpful to be able to watch this done than to have it described in words. Brushing on a glaze is appropriate where a thin coat of glaze is desired, but it must be done with care. It is easier if the pot can be placed on a whirler. A soft, squared brush is best. Load the brush with glaze and make one stroke. The glaze is quickly absorbed. Start your next stroke where the last one ended. Continue in this way round and round the pot until it is covered. If a thicker coat of glaze is required, another application

Fig. 65

with perpendicular brush strokes can be made. Further application, using the same technique, can be made diagonally.

To glaze a plate, hold the rim with three finger-tips of each hand, slide under the glaze and when you bring it out, twist from side to side as you tip it to drain off the surplus glaze (see fig. 65 bottom).

Spraying glaze is not usually done by the studio potter, since the result is necessarily mechanical. There are other reasons for not spraying. Lead, much used in glaze, can be poisonous if not handled with care. It is necessary where people are employed, or in Art Schools, that a proper spraying booth is installed. This has a screen and a fan which takes away the excess glaze. In the hands of a single studio potter red and white leads need commonsense precautions. Do not breathe the dust from lead when weighing it: a mask is easily improvised. Do not eat or smoke when mixing lead glazes. See that you have no open cuts on your hands. Wash your hands when glaze work is completed.

Lead can be used in the form of frit, i.e. lead bisilicate, which meets the Ministry of Education's requirements. Studio potters usually prefer the raw material—it seems to fit the clay better.

When your work is glazed handle it as little as possible. Look over each piece carefully to ensure that it is done to the best of your ability. If you are not satisfied, wash off and dip again. You must wait until all surface moisture has disappeared before you dip. If the glaze then looks thin, you can dip once more, but do this while the surface of the first coat is still damp for it will adhere better.

Glazing over underglaze painting needs to be nice and even if the design beneath is to be seen to advantage. Rub away any bumps in the glaze with your fingers. Smooth away pin holes, if any, or touch with a spot of glaze on a brush. Grease on a pot will prevent glaze adhering and must be removed before attempting to glaze.

That brings me to resist decoration, which as we have seen is achieved by painting on the biscuited pot with liquid wax. When the design is complete, dip in the intended glaze. The wax will burn out in the firing, giving a matt design on a glazed ground. If liked, colour can be brushed on (at the same time as the wax design) and then glazed.

Economy of line makes a beautiful decoration in this dish made at Wenford.
(*Victoria and Albert Museum*)

PLATE 13

The elegance of this bowl lies in its lovely brushwork by an obviously very practised hand. Underglaze painted in black on buff body. A line of blue paint is a background for the frieze of fishes on the inside rim. It is Persian from Kasham, early thirteenth century.

PLATE 14

Many interesting effects can be obtained with resist work and individual styles can be developed.

Practice will give you the dexterity that glazing requires. In really deft hands a large number of pots can be glazed in a surprisingly short time.

IO

To Those Wishing to Mix Their Own Glazes

To mix your own glaze it is necessary to understand something of the nature of the materials you will be using. Man discovered some of them as long ago as 5000 B.C. and, as he knew no chemistry, the materials must have become obvious to him. Glaze may have been discovered by accident. Man would have been quick to notice the effect of a glaze. The discovery of glaze was a great advance on the previous frequently low-fired ware unable to hold liquid for any length of time. Porous ware, however, is still used in hot countries for it keeps the liquid inside cool. On my table at the moment of writing there is a low-fired jar containing water standing in a glazed bowl. The jar is of ancient pattern. The bowl it stands in takes the leakage and the water in the jar remains cool.

We are concerned now with the glazed bowl in which the jar stands. This is an earthenware bowl such as you will be making and firing from about 960° C. to 1100° C.

Glaze is a melt of earthy materials. Clay itself contains these materials.

The most important ingredient of glaze is silica. Silica would form a glass by itself if taken to a high enough temperature. For our purpose it is necessary to lower the melting point of silica. This is done by adding what is called a "flux" in the form of a metal oxide. China clay (alumina) is added to thicken the glaze as it melts, preventing it from running off the surface of rounded pots. This quality in glaze is referred to as the "viscosity". Glaze, then, is composed of silica, flux and alumina.

Your glaze experiments must be carried out as scientifically as possible. It would be depressing to make a beautiful glaze and then realise that you had no idea how it was obtained. You must be prepared to make many experiments and the results of these must be recorded meticulously. Keep a log. Test tiles must be made and these are better not flat, since you will want to know the viscosity of the glaze you are mixing, so if you throw a plate with an upward, inward slanting side, it can be cut in sections when leather-hard and will give you suitable surfaces for experiments.

You will need scales for weighing out your materials—these must be accurate and it is usual to weigh in grammes—and a pestle and mortar if you are grinding your own raw materials. A glass slab and spatula are useful for mixing very small amounts for tests. There is a more expensive piece of equipment called a ball mill. This is a cylinder of porcelain filled about two-thirds full of flint pebbles. The glaze materials are placed in this with some water, the electric power is switched on and the jar rotates. It rotates just fast enough for the pebbles to fall continually from the sides of the jar and so grind the materials. You do not need to buy one of these unless you are going to produce quite a lot of pottery and are particularly interested in glaze. Some kitchen electric mixers can be used to mix glaze, providing the materials being used are not too coarse.

Glazes are usually known by the names of their fluxes and are called alkaline, boracic and lead. There is usually more than one oxide present, but that which is present in the greatest quantity gives its name to the glaze.

The oxides used as fluxes produce a clear colourless glaze, with the exception of lead which adds a faint warm yellow tone. Lead is very typical of English slipware.

The colouring oxides are usually added in small amounts. If the added flux of the colouring oxide is enough to affect the viscosity of the glaze, it can be compensated by an increase of alumina.

Alkaline glazes

These give the most intense colours. The earliest glazes are thought to have originated in Egypt and I expect you are all familiar with the beautiful turquoise blue of early Egyptian beads and small ornaments. The colour was obtained from copper oxide; the desert sand would provide silica and sodium and potassium would be readily available. An alkaline glaze is two parts of silica, which can be in the form of white sand, plus one part of the flux of potassium or sodium or both. There are, however, great difficulties in using the materials raw. Some of the ingredients are soluble in water. This means that the exact amount of water must be added, for you cannot let the glaze settle and pour some water off the top since you will lose some ingredients. Also, on porous ware where glaze is absorbed quickly, the water permeates the pot, carrying some of the ingredients with it and upsetting the glaze composition. These difficulties are overcome by using a fritted glaze.

A fritted glaze is one in which the materials have been put together and fired to a temperature at which they fuse and become glassy. This is taken out of the kiln while still hot, plunged into cold water to shatter it and then ground to a fine powder. It is possible for you to do this yourself by putting the materials into an old biscuited pot that has been given a good coat of flint wash. Fire to about 980°C. Break out of the pot while still hot and drop into cold water, and grind the resulting pieces of glass.

You can by-pass this effort by buying an alkaline frit from the glaze merchants. It is for you to decide whether you are so interested in glaze that you wish to make your own frits.

To prepare an alkaline glaze from a bought alkaline frit, use 85 parts alkaline frit, 10 parts of china clay and 5 parts of whiting. Mix with water to a creamy consistency and sieve through a 100 mesh lawn before using. Temperature is important with alkaline glazes—there is not so much allowance for overstepping. This is because the fluxes are strong and you may find your glaze too fluid, in which case add more clay. On the other hand, if it is too stiff, reduce the amount of clay.

If you do decide to use raw glazes, they must be ground, mixed with just the right amount of water and used at once on a hard biscuit, or one made less porous by an application of gum tragacanth. Do not save any glaze which is left over.

Here is a recipe for a raw glaze without making a frit:

> 31   parts soda ash
> 10·5 parts whiting
> 12   parts flint
> 55·5 parts feldspar

Grind these materials with a pestle and mortar. Pass them in the dry state through a 100 mesh lawn, mix with just the right amount of water, adding a little at a time, to the consistency of thin cream. Use at once, keeping the mixture stirred. If you dip in a finger and your nail is immediately coated with glaze, it is right.

Some people think raw glazes are best brushed on: why not try brushing and dipping to see which you prefer?

Do not keep glaze on your hands for long, since some ingredients are caustic. Rubber gloves are rather too clumsy, but glazing is quite quick work, so wash your hands afterwards.

Boracic glazes

Boric oxide is a strong flux for low-temperature glazes and favours the development of blues and greens, the warm colours from iron being more subdued.

Boric oxide comes from the supplier in the form of Boracic acid or borax. These materials are soluble in water and you can see, therefore, that the same difficulties are encountered as with alkaline glazes. There is, however, an insoluble form and this is in a natural mineral of colemanite or borocalcite. The following glaze is raw boracic and must be ground and used at once, as explained previously:

24 parts borocalcite
24 parts barium carbonate
42 parts feldspar
12 parts flint

This glaze is intended for a hard earthenware temperature for firing about 1060°C., but you must be prepared to experiment. Small tests placed near the spy-hole of the kiln may be hooked out with a wire and examined—but make sure that these tests do not get in the way of your view of the cones (see page 97). Made in ring form, with one flat side on which to stand, they will show the viscosity of the glaze if it is painted over the rounded top. See that there is kiln wash under them: you must not spoil your kiln shelves.

Boracic frits are available which, with additions of clay and flint, feldspar or whiting, make good low-temperature glazes. A frit has already been fired to a glass and would make a glaze by itself, but it would be too fluid for your purpose; hence these additions of clay to thicken and flint to harden and allow for it to be taken to a higher temperature. There is a field for experiment here, but you must be systematic in your adding of percentages until you arrive at a good glaze base. After this, you can experiment further with additions of tin, whiting or zinc oxide.

The supplier will suggest additions of stone and clay to a given frit. You can experiment by using two frits together with additions. There is infinite scope.

Lead glazes

When lead was first discovered as a glaze material, there were great advances in glazed ware. The earliest examples came from Syria and Babylonia, where walls of palaces were decorated with tiles. There are some examples in the British Museum of architectural tiles used in the palace of Darius at Susa. The metal oxides for colouring the glazes have been handled with considerable taste.

The use of lead became universal. It spread to China and to Europe, where it came into general use for all peasant pottery.

Lead is a strong flux at earthenware temperatures. It fits the clay easily and is not subject to faults in the firing. In medieval England lead sulphide (or galena) was dusted straight on to the raw damp clay pots and dishes through a coarse linen bag. This produced a glaze when fired. Galena has the advantage of not being poisonous. You could try this today, but only where the firing is done in an open up-draught kiln, since a good supply of oxygen is necessary during firing.

Red and white lead (lead oxide and lead carbonate) are poisonous and must not be used in classes where there are young people or where pottery is being commercially produced. I have mentioned this in the previous chapter. The small amount of lead used by the single studio potter could not be called dangerous, but the precautions mentioned previously are called for. Glaze well handled is a quick process and the time in contact with the materials is small.

You can make your first experiment with lead glaze this way: take two parts of lead oxide to one part of the earthenware clay you are using, plus one part of fine sand. Mix with water to a light creamy consistency and paint on to your test tiles. This will fire to a smooth shiny glaze, amber to reddish-brown in colour (according to the amount of iron in your clay). Just such a glaze was used by peasant potters in the last century, maturing somewhere between cones 010–04 or 900° C.–1020° C.

Lead is also used in the form of frits—lead bisilicate, lead monosilicate, lead sesquisilicate and litharge. Lead bisilicate meets the Ministry of Education's requirements for use in schools. White lead is more frequently used than red lead, since the latter has rather coarse particles and the red colour restricts the glaze colour. A rather more complicated glaze could be made like this:

50 parts white lead
20 parts frit
10 parts feldspar
10 parts whiting
10 parts clay

Flint adds hardness to a glaze and enables the firing temperature to be raised. Feldspar is the most useful of glaze materials and, in this case, it adds some flux. The whiting also adds hardness and the clay is for ease of application and to slow down the melt.

If, when fired, this glaze appears dull and the surface is rough, it is because there is not enough flux; therefore increase the lead. If the glaze has tended to run, being too fluid, then the hardening materials such as flint, clay and whiting must be increased. It is quite possible with a few tests to arrive at a workable glaze at the temperature you require. This is how the old craftsmen worked.

These glazes given are all clear and are intended to be weighed in grammes to give a small amount suitable for a few pieces or tests.

Glazes may also be opaque, matt, shiny or crystalline. Tin oxide may be added to a lead glaze to make it opaque and suitable for majolica decoration. About 5 per cent will be enough to make most glazes opaque. Zirconium oxide may be used instead of tin oxide; it is considerably cheaper but rather more must be used to obtain the same degree of opacity.

If you want a completely white glaze, 12 per cent of zirconium oxide will give it to you, but it may be rather harsh compared with tin glaze and some of the colours are not so pleasant. A semi-opaque glaze, that is, with about half the amount of opacifier, gives some very interesting effects over slips and painted decorations which are mysteriously half revealed through the glaze.

A warning about zirconium: do not use it with chrome or you may get unwanted colours of pink and brown.

Matt glazes are also opaque. Small crystals forming on the surface of the glaze will cause it to be matt, which is really the best kind. Mattness can be obtained by overloading with alumina (clay) or whiting. Alumina causes the glaze to be somewhat underfired at the intended temperature and, therefore, matt.

Barium oxide gives a particularly attractive matt quality in a lead glaze.

Rutile can also be used, but this adds some colour of iron since it is

93

an ore containing titanium oxide and iron oxide and can produce a mottled colour in an otherwise smooth glaze. Rutile is rather a favourite with studio potters, for it gives beautifully soft colours and interesting texture. Try 5 per cent and note the effect. Matt glazes must be quite thickly applied.

The information I have given you is meant as a starting point for those of you wishing to experiment. Some of you reading this may want to study glaze much further. To you I recommend a book by Daniel Rhodes called *Clay and Glazes for the Potter*. In this book he explains how to originate glazes, using the molecular formula.

Artistic quality, however, is not necessarily the result of greater knowledge and those of you without scientific bent need feel no dismay. You can look back in wonder at the beauty of a Chun glaze and feel that the potter knew and loved the simple materials with which he worked. He understood their properties, without being aware of chemistry. To quote from an eighteenth-century American slipware plate, "Out of earth with understanding the potter makes everything."

Glaze faults

A common fault with glaze is crazing. This is a network of cracks in the glaze surface. If you take pots out of the kiln before they are really cool, they will craze from shock. You will hear tinkling sounds as craze lines appear and you will never want to make this mistake again. In this case, there may be nothing wrong with the glaze which, if given the right treatment, will behave normally.

When a glaze cools after firing it contracts, and if it contracts more than the body a tension is set up, with the result that the glaze no longer fits the clay and splits up in a network of cracks. This may be obvious to you when you take the ware from the kiln. Craze lines may appear days and sometimes a week or two later. This suggests that the body was not mature and needed to be taken to a higher temperature.

The first remedy to try for crazing is an addition of flint to the glaze. A small amount may be added to the body. If this does not prove a cure, try reducing the feldspar. You can try reducing the soda and

94

Lead glazed earthenware dish from East Persia, ninth or tenth century A.D. Note the interesting and beautifully spaced design. This decoration should have been an inscription, but perhaps our potter was a better artist than scholar, for as an inscription it is illegible, as a design exquisite.

(*Victoria and Albert Museum*)

PLATE 15

Top left, author at the wheel; *top right*, a built jar in the form of a cockerel, a pepper pot and a built casserole; *bottom left*, more examples of the author's work; *bottom right*, part of a mural decoration: four different clays have been used as body and slip, inset in plaster, and it has also been carved.

PLATE 16

potash content, adding boric oxide. Increasing alumina may help. You can use lead instead of soda and potash.

Of course, if you are intent on the strong colours of a high alkaline glaze, you may have to accept some craze lines as inevitable. This does not matter where the ware is for a purely decorative purpose. For useful ware, crazing is not practical, for it is necessarily porous at certain temperatures. The Chinese have used crazing as a decorative feature beautifully, but this is on stoneware and porcelain where the temperatures of firing are much higher and the clay body is vitreous and non-porous.

In the higher temperature range the glazes become simpler in composition, more muted in colour, but have a quality all their own. When you have mastered the problems of low-temperature pottery, you may care to try stoneware, but this book is concerned with earthenware.

Scaling and peeling   This glaze flaw is the opposite of crazing. The glaze is under considerable compression which causes it to buckle and peel away from the clay body. The remedies are the reverse of those for crazing. Reduce the flint in the glaze, and in the body if necessary, and increase feldspar and alkaline materials in the glaze.

Crawling occurs when the glaze moves during firing, leaving bare patches of clay. It may happen in just one or two places, or it may gather in blobs and may even run off the ware in droplets on to the kiln shelves. This may be due to dirt on the biscuited ware. Grease, from being much handled, will cause this. See that ware is quite clean before glazing; wash if necessary. You may need to add more gum to the glaze slip. If the glaze, when dried, has cracks, this could cause crawling. See that all cracks are smoothed over with a finger so that they are filled with dry glaze. If underglaze painting has been heavy and is piled up, the glaze may crawl away from this. Underglaze colour should be applied more thinly and gum added to the colour. Reduce the clay content of the glaze or use calcined clay.

Blistering This is inclined to happen to lead glazes if the atmosphere in the kiln becomes reduced. This means that there is a lack of oxygen in the kiln and the atmosphere becomes smoky, or flames from burners come in contact with the ware. This does not happen in electric kilns where the atmosphere is constantly an oxidising atmosphere. Blisters can be caused by the presence of sulphur in the clay body. This can be cured by the addition of small amounts of barium carbonate to the clay. Glaze will blister if applied too thickly. This happens sometimes on the inside of bowls. Another cause is an uneven firing cycle.

The commonest faults in "glost" firing are under-firing and over-firing. In under-firing the glaze may be rough and harsh; a second firing at a higher temperature may save the situation.

Over-fired ware sometimes produces quite unexpected, even satisfying results. On the other hand, the glaze may run off the top portion of the ware and be thick at the base or stuck to the kiln shelf; or it may collapse.

Good, even potting, well-applied glaze, careful checking of glaze ingredients, a well-packed kiln and steady firing cycle will lead to good results.

I I

Firing

Temperature is the vital point in successful firing. The maturing point of the clay used must be known, or discovered if it has been dug by the potter. If you have bought your clay you will know from the supplier the maturing temperature. Well-fired clay has a ring to it when tapped; a dull, chalky sound means under-firing. A soft biscuit is easier to glaze, and for classes of youngsters this may be an advantage since glaze application will not be easy to them.

It will be necessary to have some indication of the temperature being reached inside the kiln. This is done by means of "cones". These are little pyramids of glaze materials, so graded that they will bend over by reason of the heat at given temperatures. For "soft biscuit" firing one cone would do, but if you are going to "hard biscuit" it is best to have three and fix them in line as shown in fig. 66. They are prepared by making a little stand for them of fireclay or ordinary clay, giving the clay time to dry before the firing. Packing the kiln

Fig. 66

for biscuit firing is simpler than packing for a "glost" or glaze firing.

Range your pots on a table close to the kiln and survey the situation. Note the sizes of the pieces to be fired. Take into consideration that the cones must come opposite the spy-hole where they can be seen easily. The kiln fires better if well and evenly filled. If you have one very large piece it may be more practical to save it till you have others

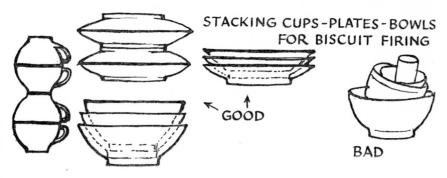

STACKING CUPS-PLATES-BOWLS
FOR BISCUIT FIRING

GOOD

BAD

Fig. 67

of a similar size, or space may be wasted. Biscuit pots can be placed one inside another providing the weight is well distributed. Beware of shrinkage; do not fill a large jar with smaller things that cannot, after the large jar has shrunk, be withdrawn through the neck. Plates can

97

stack three deep if the foot rings are placed one over the other. In this way they will not distort. The same applies to bowls. Cups may be stacked rim to rim if very evenly potted.

Before you actually start packing the kiln, decide which is your tallest pot for the kiln floor. Now place your props for the next shelf. You will then know how much floor space you have. Thick ware is best placed in the bottom of the kiln. The props are interlocking, and pieces can be added to build up to the required height. All this kiln "furniture", as it is called, is made from high-fired clay and therefore it will not warp at the temperature in your kiln.

Fig. 68   A packed kiln for biscuit firing

You will not need much in the way of shelves for the biscuit firing, but for the glost, where no two things must touch, you will need more. I suggest that three or four would be enough for a medium-sized kiln. Some that are half the kiln area would also be useful. Potters working regularly naturally want to take full advantage of their kiln space, and things made in sets, such as mugs, cups, plates and jugs, can fill the kiln to capacity at each firing, making it economic.

Ware should be placed at least 1½ in. away from the elements.

When you are satisfied that you have packed the base of the kiln to best advantage, carefully lower the next shelf on to the props, and continue. When the kiln is completely packed, place your cones opposite the spy-hole (where, in bending, they cannot touch anything), close the door and firing can begin.

The cones are spaced at intervals of 10° or 20° C. The first one bends and acts as a warning. The second is the temperature you intend to reach and the last must not be allowed to fall. In this way you know just what the temperature is in your kiln. There is a much more expensive piece of electrical equipment you can buy, called a Pyrometer, which will give you the temperature inside your kiln. In this case you read the temperature from a dial placed on the wall near your kiln. Seger cones, however, are very inexpensive and keep you watching your kiln with care. When you become very experienced, you will know, by the look of the colour in the kiln, the temperature you are approaching. Never guess, however; rely on the cones which have been proved trustworthy.

Your kiln is now ready; all that remains is to switch on to start the firing. Whatever kiln you buy you will receive firing instructions from the maker. There will be three heats on your electric kiln, "low", "medium" and "high". A large kiln may have the switches duplicated. Switch to "low". This starts what is known as the "smoking" period. Although you may think that the pots are perfectly dry when you put them in the kiln, there is really quite a lot of moisture still in them. This moisture must now be driven off and this must be done slowly if the pots are to be safe. The bung must be left out until there is no evidence of moisture. Usually this takes about two hours, but it varies according to the size of kiln and the amount and thickness of ware inside. If the bung is in the top of the kiln, a small mirror held over the top will show you, by steaming, if there is still moisture in the kiln. If the bung is in the door, a metal rod will act in the same way.

Once your bung is in, the temperature will start to build up, but this first phase is slow. It is impossible for me to give you the time taken for a firing, since there will be too many variations in sizes of kilns and contents. I will, however, give you some information which was given to me by an electric kiln maker. He said that the best and cheapest heat is when on "low", as the kiln lining is not being subjected to extremes of temperature or thermal shock. When the temperature reaches 650°–700° or even 800° C., turn to "medium" for thirty minutes. Do not leave on "medium" for long as the elements are now firing alternately. Then switch to "high" until 900° C. is reached. At this point the switches are turned to "low" for fifteen minutes. This allows the heat to come out of the lining and to soak into the ware. This should be done every 100° until you reach your intended temperature. By this means your elements are not put to a strain and will last longer. This may sound over-cautious, but you will be able to speed it up when you are more experienced.

Elements will eventually burn out and have to be replaced, but if by careful treatment you can make them last, so much the better since they are rather expensive. It would be as well to inquire the price of replacements when inquiring about electric kilns.

When the second cone bends (fig. 69) in your kiln, switch off the heat. Now seal round the door and spyhole with a roll of fireclay and leave to cool. It is usual to leave the kiln to cool for the same time as it took to fire. Take out the bung first, then open the door a little and leave for half an hour before opening fully. The ware will still be hot. Some people use asbestos gloves for removing ware from the kiln, but I take the view that these are unnecessary. If the ware is too hot to touch, don't! Leave it to cool.

Fig. 69

Glost firing

The procedure for glost firing requires much more care in preparation. First, the kiln furniture must be painted over with kiln wash. This is a mixture of equal parts of flint and china clay, mixed to a creamy consistency with water. Paint the top surfaces of shelves only; if painted underneath bits might flake off and spoil your glazes on the lower shelves. The object of this painting is to protect your shelves from drips of glaze that may run in firing. They are more easily re-moved with a chisel if shelves have been flint washed. Shelves should have a good surface. It helps if you dust them with a little flint or sand or "pitchers", which is a grog made from high-fired porcelain. If you use these materials, you must be very careful that none gets on your glazed surfaces or these will be spoilt. Pack your shelves with care so that none falls from the top shelf on to things beneath.

Most studio potters clear the foot rings of their pots from glaze. It is also quite usual to bare the glaze a little up the side of the pot. This allows for the glaze to run in the melt. Some glazes, especially those thickly applied, may run more in the melt. This quality of being runny or thick in the melt is known as the "viscosity" of a glaze. You will soon get to know the glazes with which you are work-ing, and will allow for them or change them as you see fit.

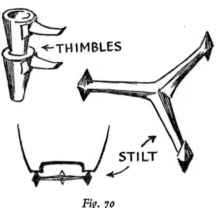

If you wish to glaze your ware all over, it will be necessary to support it on small refractory points (fig. 70). These points or stilts can be bought cheaply from suppliers. You can make your own from fireclay, but it is

Fig. 70

hardly worth while unless it is for some particular piece. These supports have three small points. The glaze should not stick to these, which should fall away as the ware cools. If they do not do so, you must hit them sharply with a mallet. There will be three small scars left, and if pieces of glaze are standing up from the scars they must be filed away, since they will be dangerous to the fingers. These are best ground off by a fast-running stone wheel. Carborundum can be used, but it is inclined to scratch the glaze.

Supports called thimbles make it possible to stack plates and saucers one above another (see fig. 70). You will see this kiln furniture illustrated in the suppliers' catalogues, and must buy according to your needs.

It would be wise to put your lead glazed ware on one shelf. Lead glaze can become volatile at certain temperatures and may affect other glazes. Separate chrome from tin glazed ware, or your white tin glaze could be tinged with pink. Experience will soon teach you the behaviour of the glazes with which you are working.

Fig. 71 Kiln packed for glaze firing

When your kiln is completely packed, put the cones in place (fig. 71). Be careful that they are not near a cherished pot so that they can touch it when they bend.

For the first three-quarters of an hour the heat must be low. After this, the heat can be raised steadily to the required temperature. Glost firing is much quicker than a bisque or biscuit firing, since the clay has already been subjected to heat.

When the required temperature has been reached, the kiln is sealed and allowed to cool for the same time as it took to fire. Do not take out your glazed ware if it is too hot to touch or there may be crazing of the glaze. It is a great moment when you open the kiln and see the result of your efforts.

The wise beginner will keep a log of firings, with notes of temperatures and times taken to reach them, and also notes on differences in glazes in relation to their placing in the kiln. It will then be possible to repeat a desired effect. By studying your log you will soon get to know your kiln well and this is most necessary since it is your most vital piece of equipment. Careful application of glazes and a well-packed glost kiln will help towards success.

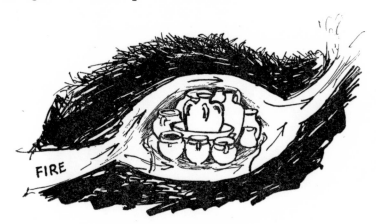

Fig. 72 Roman bank kiln

Man has fired his pots from ancient times. Perhaps his kilns were not very efficient or economical on fuel, but his work is still before our eyes to prove his skill. Even today, in parts of Africa, pottery is biscuit-fired in an open bonfire.

Perhaps some of you reading this book will have seen that remarkable potter from Nigeria, Ladi Kwali, who demonstrated on television how to pull up a large pot from a single lump of clay without the help of a wheel. Our own well-known potter, Michael Cardew, has taught the Nigerians how to glaze their ware, using kilns, but the bonfire is still used where kilns are not available.

What an interesting experiment a bonfire firing would be for a class of children in a country school, or for a large family or group of children. It will be extra satisfying if the clay has been locally dug. The clay must be a strong type, containing sand and grog, so that it will stand up to rapidly applied heat. Of course, the pots will be of varying colours when fired, according to their position in the fire. Some will be red, some blackened with smoke, some variegated. This

Fig. 73 Bonfire firing

is not necessarily a defect—it may add to the artistic quality, especially when nicely decorated in the clay state. There may be some breakages, but there will also be successes, and plenty of excitement in building the bonfire and even more when it is unpacked. Children will enjoy collecting wood for this venture.

Not too much space is needed and it can be done on the hard surface of a cobbled yard or on the soft earth of a garden. Soft earth is possibly easier. A round, shallow shape is dug and a bed of fairly fine sticks is arranged as the spokes of a wheel. Let this be a good, even layer. Now arrange the pots on this. The large ones should be grouped in the middle, small ones placed round and others can be built to make a strong pile with weight well distributed.

Round the base of the dug shape must be placed materials for lighting the fire quickly and evenly, such as screwed-up newspapers and fine twigs or dried grass if available. Now comes the stouter wood of which you must have a large supply. This is built into a wigwam shape round the pile. It would be easier to dig the first lot into the soft ground to keep the shape. When these sticks are in place, you can light the fire to windward so that it will catch quickly. You must have a good pile of spare wood to keep the fire going for about three-quarters to one hour. When the last of your wood has been put on, the fire must be banked. This can be done from the base up with damp leaves, piles of weeds from gardening and, finally, a layer of earth. Leave a hole at the top to act as a chimney. The heat is now entirely enclosed, which is one of the principles of firing. The heat can now soak well into the pots.

Of course, you will have no idea of the temperature attained, but the clay will have been changed from its raw state to at least the flower-pot stage and maybe more. Heat from coniferous wood is particularly fierce and builds up a good temperature.

Be careful when the children come to unpack the fire. You can leave it to cool completely or unpack it gradually, letting the heat out slowly, for a lot is retained in a banked fire. A pair of fire tongs could be used to remove the pots.

TEMPERATURE CHART FOR FIRING

CONE	DEGREES C.	DEGREES F.	TYPE OF WARE
022	600	1112 ⎫	
021	650	1202 ⎬	Low-fired biscuit and some enamels
020	670	1238 ⎭	
019	690	1274	
018	710	1310	
017	730	1346	
016	750	1382 ⎫	Liquid gold and silver lustres
015A	790	1454 ⎭	
014A	815	1499	
013A	835	1535	
012A	855	1571	
011A	880	1616 ⎫	Lustres
010A	900	1652 ⎬	Hard enamels
09A	920	1688 ⎭	Slipware
08A	940	1724	Soft biscuit firing
07A	960	1760	Majolica glaze and decoration
06A	980	1796 ⎫	Soft glazes
05A	1000	1832 ⎭	Hard biscuit for majolica
04A	1020	1868	Soft glazes intended for earthenware fired to hard biscuit
03A	1040	1904	
02A	1060	1940	
01A	1080	1976	Hard earthenware, unglazed, and glazes for soft earthenware
1A	1100	2012	
2A	1120	2048	
3A	1140	2084	
4A	1160	2120	
5A	1180	2156	For those wishing to make their own kiln furniture from fire clay
6A	1200	2192	
7A	1230	2246	
8A	1250	2282	

Fig. 74 Mycenean sarcophagus

CERAMIC SUPPLIERS

Kilns

Applied Heat Co. Ltd.,
Elecfurn Works,
Otterspool Way,
Watford By-Pass, Watford, Herts.

Arterial Engineering Works,
40 Bowlers Croft,
Basildon, Essex.

Bricesco Electrikilns,
British Ceramic Service Co. Ltd.,
Park Avenue,
Wolstanton, Newcastle, Staffs.

Corbic,
"Bourneside",
Gomshall, Surrey.

Cromartie Kilns Ltd.,
Dividy Road,
Longton, Staffs.

Dowson & Mason Gas Plant Co. Ltd.,
Alma Works,
Levenshulme,
Manchester, 19. (Gas kilns)

Dryad Handicrafts,
Northgates, Leicester, and
Bloomsbury Street, London. (All ceramic supplies)

Arthur Homer,
Wayside Cottage,
St Agnes, Cornwall. (Supplies plans for oil-fired kilns)

Podmore & Sons Ltd.,
Shelton,
Stoke-on-Trent, Staffs. (All ceramic supplies)

Bernard W. E. Webber (Dept. F),
Phoenix Works,
Broad Street,
Hanley, Stoke-on-Trent, Staffs.

Wengers Ltd.,
Etruria,
Stoke-on-Trent, Staffs. (All ceramic supplies)

Wheels

Arden Wheel (Pottery) Co., incorporating
A. T. Hobson & Co, Engineers,
Meriden, Country Potters Equipment Co.,
73/77 Britannia Road, London, S.W.6.

Edwards & Jones Ltd.,
Longton,
Stoke-on-Trent, Staffs.

Woodleys Joinery Works,
Newton Poppleford, Devon. (Make a kick wheel as designed by
  Bernard Leach)

Refractories

(Kiln muffles, insulating bricks, kiln furniture, saggars)

Morgan Crucible Co.,
Battersea Church Road, London, S.W.11.

Acme Marls Ltd.,
Clough Street,
Hanley, Stoke-on-Trent, Staffs.

Bullers Joyners Works,
Hanley, Stoke-on-Trent, Staffs.

Hall & Pickles Ltd.,
P.O. Box 116,
Manchester, 1.

Brushes, Glazes, Clays and Chemicals

Cotton Bros.,
Crown Works,
Longton, Stoke-on-Trent, Staffs.

Tiranti,
72 Charlotte Street,
London, W.1. (All excellent modelling tools, as well as other supplies)

Sponges, Colours, Enamels, Lustres, etc.

E. W. Good & Co. (Longton) Ltd.,
Baker Street Colour Works,
Longton, Stoke-on-Trent, Staffs.

Johnson, Matthey & Co. Ltd.,
73–83 Hatton Garden,
London, E.C.1.

Clays

Fulham Pottery,
Fulham Road,
London, S.W.6.

Pike Bros.,
Poole, Dorset. (For ball clays)

Potclays Ltd.,
Wharf House,
Copeland Street,
Hanley, Stoke-on-Trent, Staffs.

English China Clay Sales Ltd.,
14 High Cross Street,
St Austell, Cornwall.

Watts, Blake & Bearn Ltd.,
Newton Abbot, Devon. (Ball clay, etc.)